SO-CFN-949

The Violin and Its Masters

By the same author

GIANTS OF THE KEYBOARD

The
VIOLIN
and
Its
MASTERS

Victor Chapin

J. B. Lippincott Company

Philadelphia   *New York*

For John and Perdita Schaffner

The author would like to thank the following for permission to use the photographs in this book: THE BETTMANN ARCHIVE; THE NEW YORK PUBLIC LIBRARY.

Contents

I

Prélude

———~———

The violin, which often has been called the aristocrat or even the king of instruments, was, during the early years of its existence, looked down upon socially. The reasons for this were complex; but to put the matter simply, the accomplished musical amateur of the sixteenth century was used to playing upon the viols and continued to do so, while the new violin, which was much more difficult to master, became the instrument of professionals, who were considered social inferiors and often performed in lowly taverns. Moreover, these professionals, at least for a while, played the violin mostly for dancing, an activity that was considered suitable for peasants but not for aristocrats. Nevertheless, frivolous or daring aristocrats did dance, though in a more formal or courtly way; and professional violinists, who could produce on their instrument sharper and more incisive rhythms than was possible on the viols, soon were employed at the courts of Europe, where they helped to make dancing increasingly popular. In the late sixteenth century, the aristocracy was both titivated and scandalized by a dance called *La Volta*, in which couples not only held each other in embrace but alternately jumped into the air. It has been claimed that Queen Elizabeth of England joined in this dance. We do know that she liked to dance and sometimes did before her court, though one wonders if she could have permitted herself to go so far as to join in the lively but—for a queen—undignified measures of *La Volta*.

If the violin and its sister instruments, the viola, cello, and double bass, were invented by any single individuals, we do not know who they were. Claims have been made for various men, including Leonardo da Vinci, but they are without foundation. It was believed for a while that the actual inventor of the violin was Gaspar Duiffoprugcar, who was born in Bavaria in 1514 and worked as a lute maker in Lyons in France, where he died in 1571. But instruments supposedly of his making were eventually discovered to be nineteenth-century forgeries.

What we do know of the evolution of the violin family is gleaned from a few documents and treatises and from pictures. The earliest-known illustration of the violin is in a fresco by Gaudenzio Ferrari, *The Madonna of the Orange Trees*, in the Italian church of San Cristoforo in Vercelli, near Milan, painted about 1529 or 1530. A later fresco by Gaudenzio in the cupola of the cathedral at Saronno depicts the violin, viola, and cello, which then employed three strings and were bowed overhand.

The development of the violin family and its relationship to older instruments is a most complex subject and one that has been confused and misunderstood for centuries. In fact, it remained for scholars of our own times to clarify matters. The most important in this field is David D. Boyden, who published his monumental study, *The History of Violin Playing from Its Origins to 1761*, in 1965. He has shown that a confusion of languages and of terms adapted from one language to another served to obscure the facts. The direct ancestors of the violin family were not, as people long assumed, the viols, but instruments that evolved but departed from them, particularly the fiddle, the rebec, and the *lira da braccio*. These instruments became obsolete by the middle of the sixteenth century, when they were replaced by the violin family. However, the viols did not become obsolete then but continued in use for two hundred years or so; for as long, in fact, as music was being composed for them. The rebecs were in existence as early as the thirteenth century and were a family that had instruments playing in the soprano, alto or tenor, and bass registers. They had no frets or soundboards and their bodies bore little resemblance to those of the violin family. However, they did have three strings, like the early violins, and were tuned in fifths. They were held at the breast or neck. The poet Milton refers to "the jocund rebecs," while Rabelais describes them as "subdued" and compares their sound to that of bagpipes.

The Renaissance fiddle went through various developments and existed in several varieties, but in its final form had five strings (one probably a drone or *bourdon*) and resembled the violin more than the soprano (or discant) rebec. The *lira da braccio,* a relative of the fiddle that evolved in the fifteenth century, was the closest to the violin in appearance, though it varied in size so that in some forms it was comparable to the viola. In its final form, it had seven strings, two of them drones. A number of hybrid instruments based on one or another of these instruments in combination were in use at the time when the violin family emerged. In particular, an instrument created from combining the rebec and the fiddle anticipated many of the qualities of the violin. We know from a treatise of 1545, *Musica Instrumentalis Deudsch* by Martin Agricola, that the rebecs and the violin family were tuned alike. The bass rebec and the violoncello appear to have differed in size, the rebec being smaller and perhaps played on the arm rather than held between the knees. The earliest violins probably had three strings, though the fourth string was added before 1556, when the violin is described as having four strings in *Epitome musical,* by Philibert Jambe de Fer, a musician who died in the St. Bartholomew massacre of 1572.

Though illustrations of the sixteenth century show the violin being played in the second or third position, it was for many years probably played mainly in the first, since the music of the time did not demand that it extend beyond that range. Music then, and for some time to come, imitated the human voice, so that the violin, the soprano instrument, was hardly required to do more than a soprano singer could and so was confined to two octaves. However, it is interesting to speculate on the question of improvisation. As violinists mastered their new instrument, they must have suspected its potential and perhaps explored it in improvisation (for dancing, in taverns, at fairs), even though composers continued to require less of them than they could perform.

The violin, which undoubtedly was of Italian creation, did not at once become the instrument that it is today. The sixteenth-century violin varied in size, had three strings (until the E string was added), and greatly differed in bridge, neck, and fingerboard. The pitch was different and *vibrato* was unknown except as a special effect. The early violas appear to have had a stronger tone; and when instruments were first joined in concert with voices in polyphonic music, probably by Giovanni Gabrieli in the late sixteenth century, the viola rather than the violin was employed together with wind instruments. Concerted instrumental music of this period merely copied vocal music, supporting it or occasionally imitating it. The first music for the violin that has survived in manuscript dates from 1582 and is part of a court entertainment, the *Ballet comique de la reine* (also known as *Circe*), an elaborate and costly production given by Henri III of France in 1581 to celebrate the marriage of his favorite, the Duc de Joyeuse, to the Queen's sister, Mlle. de Vaudemont. The *maître de ballet* was Balthasar de Beaujoyeulx, the leader of the band of violinists brought to the French court from Italy in about 1555. Beaujoyeulx (whose name originally was Baldassare da Belgiojoso) was called "the best violinist in Christendom" and probably is the first of the long line of famous violin virtuosos. It may have been he who was responsible for the commission by the French king, Charles IX, of a large number of violins (as many as thirty, perhaps) from Italian instrument makers. Indeed, they may all have been made by one of the earliest of the great Cremona masters, Andrea Amati.

It was Francis I of France whose interest in the arts and passion for all things Italian (including the costly and doubtful passion to conquer Milan) resulted in the importation to the French court of many Italian musicians, dancers, and artists (including Leonardo da Vinci). When Francis died in 1571, his successor, Henri II, had for his queen the notorious (and to some extent maligned) Catherine de Médicis, who, being Italian and with excellent taste, continued to patronize Italian musicians. She gave elaborate court entertainments, modeled after those of her native city of Florence, where the *intermedio,* a musico-dramatic performance that had been evolved there, soon was to develop into opera.

Though the violin of this period was a stronger instrument than any of its predecessors, it was by no means as strong an instrument as it is today. Many differences account for this, including the use of gut (sometimes silvered) instead of steel for strings and, most particularly, differences in the construction and use of the bow. The bow was not perfected or standardized until the end of the eighteenth century, and so there were bows of many shapes and sizes in use. The question of how to grip the bow finally developed two distinct answers in the form of the French grip and the Italian grip. The French grip, with the thumb under the hair, appears to have served better with a short bow and was most effective in dance music, while the Italian grip, with the thumb between the hair and the stick, was employed with a longer bow. There were variations, of course.

By the beginning of the seventeenth century, the violin family was well established. In 1601, a professional violinist named G. B. Jacomelli changed his name to G. B. Violino, which indicates that violinists must have been in demand. At the same time, the first of the great violin makers of Cremona were at work and already well known. In fact, the phenomenon had commenced some years before with Andrea Amati and Gasparo da Salò (who was not of Cremona but of Brescia). Gasparo was born about 1542 and died in 1609.

The claim, once advanced, that he was the inventor of the
violin is exploded by dates, since the evidence shows that the
violin existed before he was born. Though he was chiefly a
maker of viols, he did make some instruments of the violin
family, and a viola of c. 1580 can be seen in the Ashmolean
Museum at Oxford. He also made a hybrid instrument called
a *lira-viola* that combined features of the *lira da braccio* and
the viola. Amati, thirty years or so older than Casparo and
the first of the masters of Cremona, has also been mentioned
as the possible inventor of the violin. In his case, the claim
can not be entirely rejected, though no one has yet been able
to substantiate it.

Instrument makers went on making viols as well as instruments of the violin family, since both types were in demand. By the end of the sixteenth or beginning of the seventeenth century, a clear distinction had developed between
the *viola da gamba* and *viola da braccio,* thus separating
once and for all instruments that no longer had much in
common. The viols were played between the knees or on the
lap and had a reedy sound quite distinct from that of the
violin, viola, and cello.

The history of the great instrument makers of Cremona
would require a book all to itself. The important facts in this
context can be stated simply. The instruments of the violin
family superior to all others and for which today enormous
sums are paid were all made between 1550 and 1743 in the
Italian city of Cremona by the three Stradivari, the four
Amati, and the four Guarneri. When these great lines died
out, their skills and secrets were lost to the world, presumably forever. Many have tried, and with some small success,
to recreate these instruments, but nobody yet has produced a
violin that any player would willingly accept as a substitute
for his Stradivarius, Amati, or Guarnerius. There were, in
truth, fine instrument makers in other places, particularly
Venice and Germany, but their instruments today do not
have the reputation of those of Cremona. Only two pupils of
the last Stradivari, Antonio, managed after his death in 1737
to carry on the work successfully. But confusion about the

attribution of their instruments obscured those of Carlo Bergonzi and Domenico Montagnana, which often were credited to Stradivari or the last Guarneri, Giuseppe Antonio Guarneri de Gesù, who died about 1743. As a result of the Cremona phenomenon, which lasted just under two hundred years, the competition among players and collectors to acquire the something less than two thousand instruments that have survived is both intense and extraordinarily expensive. Fortunately, the history of music records many generous gestures on the part of patrons and collectors who have given or loaned precious instruments to players of great ability. And even more fortunately, the greatest virtuosos have been sufficiently rewarded so that they could acquire, on their own, instruments worthy of their gifts.

Though the master instrument makers of Cremona eventually outstripped all others in reputation, there were, at various times and in various places, other artists who produced fine instruments that were much in demand and some of which are still in use. These include in the seventeenth century, G. P. Maggini of Brescia; the French masters of Mirecourt, particularly Vuillaume; the Austrian, Jacob Stainer; and Nicholas Matters in England; in the eighteenth century, the Carcassi brothers of Florence; the dalla Costa brothers of Treviso; the Testore family of Milan; the Gagliani of Naples; and the Guadagni of Piacenza and Turin; Matthys Hohmans of Holland; the Klotz family of Bavaria; Nicolas Lupot of France; and Daniel Parker, Peter Walmsley, and the Hill family in England; in the late nineteenth century, the Russian A. I. Lemon, one of the most successful of modern instrument makers.

Someone—half in jest but with some truth—once described the history of music as "the survival of the loudest." As far as the evolution of instruments is concerned, stronger and therefore louder potentials became desirable as a result of certain social conditions. As long as music was performed in the small salons of the aristocracy without the presence of what we today think of as a large audience, the existing instruments of the Middle Ages (the viols, lutes, and keyboard

instruments of limited capacity such as the virginals)
sufficed. Greater effects were needed for church music, but
the organ and massed voices took care of them. In the Renaissance, elaborate court entertainments, performed for several hundred or even, occasionally, several thousand people,
became fashionable. Large ballrooms were added to old palaces or built as part of new ones. And, most importantly,
theaters, which had been known to the Greeks and Romans,
but because of religious disapproval and the physical and social restrictions of feudal society, became unknown in Christian Europe, began to appear again. Not that theatrical performances had entirely disappeared. Mystery plays, given in
churches or in the squares before them, were an important
part of medieval ritual. Dancing before the altars was a commonplace in early medieval times, and the Church experienced some difficulty in suppressing it. The practice survived only in the rarest and most privileged instances, such
as the celebrated dance of the *Seises*, which to this day is
performed once a year, during Holy Week, in the Cathedral
of Seville.

The secular entertainments that emerged in Renaissance
times as a result of a more relaxed point of view on the part
of both Church and State always employed music, as in the
masques popular at the English court and the *intermedi*
given at the Medici court in Florence. The *commedia
dell'arte* came into fashion as an entertainment for the
common people and in various forms spread throughout Europe. In England and even in America it developed into the
Punch and Judy shows so popular with children.

During the sixteenth century, the new demand for secular
entertainments brought about the establishment of two great
art forms, opera and ballet, both of which have their basis in
music. Scholars still argue about whether or not opera really
evolved from the *intermedi* or was created independently of
them. Be that as it may, the *stile representivo*, which favored
melodic expressiveness at the expense of traditional polyphony, evolved in Florence in the early years of the sixteenth
century. It soon developed into the *ricente titallitone*, the

first invention of the new operatic form, in which the solo voice was exploited with more elaborate and independent instrumental developments. The first opera, or the first work that we know that can be called an opera, was *Dafni*, composed wholly or in part by Jacopo Peri to a text by Ottavio Rinuccini, and produced in 1597 or perhaps as early as 1594 in Florence, probably in the *palazzo* of Count Giovanni Bardi, the leader of a band of amateur poets and musicians known as the *camerata*. Only a few fragments of Peri's music have survived, though we do have Rinuccini's text. The music to a second opera, *Eurydice*, has survived. It is by Peri with additions by Giulio Caccini and was given in Florence to celebrate the marriage of Henri IV of France to Marie de Médicis on October 6, 1600, at which the King was represented by proxy. Another form of musical entertainment, madrigal comedies, had become popular in Florence; these comedies have been called predecessors of opera, but they were strictly polyphonic and so do not truly qualify for that distinction. The first opera of any real importance was composed by Claudio Monteverdi; opera really began with his *Orfeo*, which was produced at the Gonzaga court in Mantua in 1607. When his next opera, *Arianna*, was given at court in Mantua on May 28, 1608, it supposedly was heard by six thousand people. The most enduring Monteverdi opera, *L'Incoronazione di Poppea*, was not composed for another thirty-four years and was produced in Venice, where by this time there were theaters in abundance. Monteverdi died a year later, having largely created a new form and brought about profound changes that affected the development of music in all its aspects.

2

Jean-Baptiste Lully

c. 1633–1687

Though an Italian and a Florentine, Jean-Baptiste Lully, born Giovanni Battista Lulli, became more French than the French and was the man who, in music, satisfied the French passion for transforming everything they borrowed from other countries into something authentically French.

He was not, it seems, a nice man. But he rose from the humblest beginnings and is of the first importance in the history of French music. The exact date of his birth is in dispute, though it generally is given as 1633, the year of Claudio Monteverdi's death. The year 1639 is, perhaps, a more likely date, though there are arguments on both sides of the question. Was he thirteen or only seven when, in 1646, he was brought to Paris by the Chevalier de Guise, who had "discovered" him in Florence? Was he twenty-five or thirty-one when, in 1664, he was married and the marriage contract was witnessed by the King, the Queen, and the Queen Mother of France? Could a child of seven have been so clever at singing, dancing, and improvising naughty songs that a nobleman of France would adopt him practically at sight? Even taking into account the contested six years, his rise from scullery boy to the King's favorite was both quick and extraordinary. A convincing argument for the earlier date is that Lully never learned French correctly, spoke it with an Italian accent, and usually wrote in Italian. Presumably, a clever boy of seven could absorb a new language completely, while a boy of thirteen, clever as he might be, would have difficulties.

The Chevalier de Guise, after bringing Lully to Paris from Florence, put him in the service of "la grande Mademoiselle," who was Anne Marie Louise d'Orléans, Duchesse de Montpensier, niece of Louis XIII and cousin of the young King Louis XIV, whom she expected to marry but never did. Lully began as a scullery boy, but Mlle. de Montpensier soon was made aware of his gifts and promoted him to page. She had him tutored in music; but the boy was lacking in gratitude, or at least in discretion, for he wrote one of his scandalous poems against his patroness, who dismissed him. According to another version of the story, he did not write the poem himself but merely set it to music.

Good fortune did not end there for Lully. He soon (in 1652) secured a place at court among the King's violins and before long had become one of the King's favorite companions.

The celebrated twenty-four *violons du roy* had been "chartered" by Louis XIII but had existed earlier as twenty-two *violons ordinaires de la chambre du roy*. The first player to be known as "the king of the violins" was Louis Constantin, who was born in 1585 and died in 1657. Lully, it seems, did not think much of the King's violins, for he organized and trained another group, *les petits violons,* which began with sixteen players but later had twenty. According to Lully's pupil, Georg Muffat, they were highly disciplined and rhythmically spirited, being chiefly concerned with dance music. Lully, apparently, avoided improvised ornaments, and most if not all of his violin music could be played in the first position and did not make use of the G string. Only a few fragments of the music played by Lully's violins have survived.

Whatever Lully's faults, he must have had charm, for the King was loyal to him to the end. As a result, Lully became a power at court and the absolute dictator of all things musical there. Since violinists were still considered upstarts and somehow inferior to lutenists, organists, or keyboard players, the musicians' guild took steps to improve their lot by setting rules about apprenticeships, payments, qualifications to become "masters," and who had the exclusive right to play where. Lully gained control of these rights and amassed a fortune in graft, for he made every violinist and eventually every musician pay him a "kickback" in return for certain rights and privileges.

During the early years of the long reign of King Louis XIV, the real power in France was Cardinal Mazarin. Originally Italian from Sicily, he encouraged the importation of Italian ideas, particularly in the arts. But the new art form, opera, failed to impress the French, who were frankly bored by it. When Francesco Cavalli, the most popular opera composer of the generation after Monteverdi, was brought to Paris to compose a work to celebrate the marriage of Louis XIV to the Infanta Maria Teresa of Spain in 1660, he found himself surrounded by intrigue and hostility. Although *Serse,* the opera that was produced in the Louvre during the wedding festivities, was coldly received, Cavalli was invited back to Paris two years later to produce another opera, *Ercole amante.* By this time, Mazarin was dead and Louis XIV was already on his way to becoming *le roi soleil.* Lully, sensing what was to come, intrigued against Cavalli and undoubtedly saw to it that his opera did not succeed and he would return to Italy in disgust. A French form of opera obviously was called for; and Lully intended that no one but he would provide it. Actually, the first French opera was not composed for eleven years and was not by Lully but the composer Robert Cambert. This work, *Pomone,* with a text by the poet Pierre Perrin, was produced in 1671 and was so successful that Lully was forced upon desperate measures. He somehow managed to prevent the production of Cambert's next opera and launched such a successful cabal against him that the poor man was forced to flee to England.

Though Lully was not to launch French opera on its long and fruitful course until 1673, he was not idle in the years immediately following Louis XIV's assumption of power. He created a form of court entertainment that greatly pleased the King, who actually danced in them, as did Lully himself. The most notable of these were done in collaboration with the French playwright, Molière. These were called *comédies-ballets* and included the ever-popular *Le Bourgeois gentil-homme* and other works, such as *Le Mariage forcé* and *Pourceaugnac,* in which there were musical interludes with dancing. If Molière had not died in 1673, Lully might not have come to opera when he did, though the last work he created with Molière, *Psyche* (1671), was so close to being an opera that it almost qualifies as one.

Lully had been given the title of court composer in 1653 and in 1662 became music master to the royal family. The year before, he had become a French citizen. In 1681, six years before his death, Louis XIV made him a court secretary in order to grant him a patent of nobility. By this time, it might be said that he had earned it, for he was a prodigious worker and organizer and between 1673 and 1687 composed fifteen operas that, whatever their merits, constitute the foundation of French opera. In addition, he composed ballets, dance pieces of other kinds, pastorals, various instrumental pieces, and church music, including the *Miserere* that is one of his best works. It has been said that Lully borrowed music from other composers that he passed off as his own. If he did, this was accepted practice. We do know that he employed assistants who finished off or filled in his compositions.

The operas of Lully were composed to texts mostly written by the poet, Philippe Quinault, with whom he enjoyed a most successful collaboration. No doubt Quinault realized that he had to get on with Lully, for the King had granted

Lully a patent that assured him the exclusive right to produce opera in France. The Académie Royale de Musique, the
official name for the Paris Opéra, was founded by Lully
under the King's patronage in 1672, at which time a rival
theater was closed down by the police, thereby guaranteeing
Lully's total domination. This was after the successful production of his pastoral *pasticcio, Les Fêtes de l'Amour et de
Bacchus,* which must have convinced the King that Lully
alone could provide the kind of entertainments he wanted.
Lully did not disappoint him. He produced one lavish and
grandiose work after another, specially designed for the
court and complete with dance music, marches, interludes,
and descriptive effects in which the strings were promi-
nently employed, particularly for rhythmic effects and for
the creation of a distinctive sonority that helped to further
the atmosphere of grandeur so essential to these court
operas. But it was the overtures to these operas, composed in
a style that swept Europe as the French Overture, that were
Lully's most significant contribution. Their construction was
simple: slow, quick, slow, that is, something that could be
called a slow "movement" followed by a quick (usually
fugal) one and ending with another slow one.

Apparently, Louis XIV did not care for melody and was
interested only in quick rhythms and spectacle. If this was
so, Lully had to repress his more subtle and intimate gifts or
give expression to them only cautiously. But he undoubtedly
was the right man in the right place at the right time so far
as the King's taste and that of his court were concerned. If
Lully was the opportunist *par excellence,* he also was a
better musician than history has been willing to admit. Perhaps that is because in the prudish nineteenth century,
music critics and historians were loath to concede that a bad
character could compose good music.

The story of Lully's death is well known. On January 8,
1687, he was conducting a *Te Deum* to celebrate the King's
recovery from an illness. As was his habit, he used a long,
heavy stick for a baton with which to beat time loudly on the

floor. Having a bad temper, he whacked the stick with particular vehemence when something went wrong and struck his foot instead of the floor. An abcess developed and gradually turned into a cancerous growth. He died on March 22, after scribbling on a piece of paper the words *Bisogna morire, peccatore.*

3

Arcangelo Corelli

1653–1713

The Corelli were an old family. Though not of the nobility, they were landowners and lived in comfortable circumstances. There had been poets in the family, but never a musician before the advent of Arcangelo Corelli, who was the first real genius of the violin. Though he called himself "Il Bolognese," he actually was born in Fusignano, a town between Bologna and Ravenna, on February 17, 1653. The established facts of his early life are few and have been much elaborated by historians. Legends, most of them patently false, have abounded, for the impulse to romanticize the life of so important a figure was irresistible. Actually, Corelli appears to have been a quiet man, totally dedicated to music, who, because he was fortunate in his patron, was able to develop his great gifts logically and consistently.

One of the suppositions about Corelli's life that can not be proven is that he did not study the violin seriously until he went to Bologna, then the musical center of Italy so far as teaching was concerned, at the age of thirteen. He undoubtedly had some training from priests in his native town and in nearby Faenza. If he had received no instruction on the violin before going to Bologna, his progress there was remarkable, for he was accepted into the exacting company of the Bolognese Accademia Filarmonica at the age of seventeen. According to the history by the eighteenth-century Bolognese theoretician and teacher, the Padre Martini, Corelli studied violin first with Giovanni Benvenuti and then with Leonardo Brugnoli, one of the most celebrated of early violinists, who was particularly brilliant in improvisation.

The first half of the seventeenth century was a time of change and advancement in music. The dominance of vocal polyphony was questioned by the emergence of major-minor tonality, the rapid advance of opera, and the first tentative experiments with independent instrumental music. Giovanni Gabrieli and Claudio Monteverdi had carried the function of the orchestra beyond that of unison accompaniment to monody and shown the possibilities for more complex accompaniment. The only musical forms that existed independently of singing were those of the dance. However, during the Tudor period in England, imaginative pieces were composed for the viols and virginals, leading to later works of much sophistication, such as John Morley's *First Book of Consort Lessons* (1599) and fantasias for viols composed by William Byrd and Orlando Gibbons. But the violin itself had not yet reached England, or, if it had, had yet to make an impression.

In Italy, the violinists of the first half of the sixteenth century were more concerned with the technical than the musical or melodic possibilities of their new instrument. Perhaps this was because melody traditionally lay exclusively within the province of the human voice. Song was to be sung; and hardly anyone before Corelli suspected that the violin (and other instruments, too) could be made to sing. Still, the range of the violin quickly was expanded beyond the two-octave range of the human voice. Monteverdi and Gabrieli both composed music for violins in an extended range. About 1600, composers began to search for more abstract forms, working from the *canzona,* derived from four-part madrigals, to the free-form *capriccio,* and then, finally, to the sonata. The first sonata for violin with *basso continuo* that has survived in print was by C. P. Cima and appeared in 1610. A sonata for three violins and bass by Gabrieli was posthumously published in 1615, though it could have been composed before Cima's sonata. The *continuo,* or figured bass, which was played by a keyboard instrument or sometimes by the cello or double bass, was an essential part of instrumental music during this period and afterwards for a hundred years or so. The *continuo* provided the harmonic underpinnings. The composer simply indicated the harmonies and the *continuo* player filled them in. This was true in orchestral music, too, until the mid-eighteenth century. The violin and piano sonata that we know today, in which each instrument has an equal and independent part, was a comparatively late development. The string quartet did not evolve until the eighteenth century, though its actual invention has been attributed to Alessandro Scarlatti, who may have experimented with it during the last years of the seventeenth century. It could be said, however, that imitations of madrigals by viols approximating the soprano, alto or tenor, and bass voices constituted an early form of the string quartet.

The distinction between the *sonata da chiesa* (church sonata) and the *sonata da camera* (chamber sonata) was made early in the seventeenth century. Tarquinio Merula was one of the first to make it, followed, more importantly, by Biagio Marini, who was born about 1597 and died in 1665. Other composers of this period who wrote pioneer works for the violin include G. B. Fontana, Carlo Farina, Solomone Rossi, and G. B. Buonamente. Marini, Farina, Rossi, and Buonamente all were pupils of Monteverdi. Maurizio Cazzati, one of the founders of the Bolognese school, has been called the first great violin teacher. His pupil, G. B. Vitali, was one of Corelli's most famous contemporaries. The Vitali *Chaconne,* familiar to all violin students, was composed by his son, Tommaso Antonio Vitali.

Biagio Marini, whose music for the violin probably was the most influential upon the generation that preceded Co-

relli's, spent many years in Germany, where the first important composer for the violin was Johann Schop. Heinrich
Schütz, whose great achievement was the early development
of the oratorio, studied with Gabrieli and Monteverdi in Italy
and brought back to Germany knowledge of the new developments in violin technique. However, a German school of
violin playing did not develop until the time of J. J. Walther
and Heinrich von Biber, both of whom were a few years
younger than Lully and a few years older than Corelli. Both
Walther and Biber explored the range of the violin up to the
seventh position and employed *staccato* effects and synco-
pated bowings. Walther composed descriptive pieces to exploit his technical accomplishments, while Biber composed
more introspective works that were religiously inspired, such
as his *Mystery* or *Rosary* sonatas. Biber is best remembered
today for his experiments with the *scordatura,* or tunings of
the violin that deviate from the normal, or *accordatura.* He
employed as many as fourteen *scordatura,* or tuning vari-
ants. Some of these were greatly imaginative and anticipated
in effect, if not actually in technique, such later innovations
as the playing of octaves and tenths.

Biber and Walther were roughly contemporary with two
violin makers of the Austrian Tyrol, Matthias Albani and
Jacob Stainer, whose instruments, for a hundred years or
so, were valued above those of the Cremona masters. J. S.
Bach owned a Stainer violin, as did many other leading musicians.

In Corelli's time, violin music had become well established. Dance music and its forms had taken on a more re-
fined character as incorporated into instrumental music,
particularly the *sonata da camera,* which employed the *chaconne, gaillaird, passacaglia, allemande, follia, gigue,* and
many other traditional dance forms. The variation form also
was coming into use. However, the trio sonata for two violins
and *continuo* was the most popular form with violinists.

Though the court of Louis XIV of France was the greatest
in Europe, it did not offer much during this period to musicians because of Lully's rigid monopoly. Germany was rav-

aged by the Thirty Years War (1618–48), and England had been in the grip of the Puritanism that followed the execution of Charles I in 1649. The rule of Oliver Cromwell ended with the restoration of Charles II in 1660, but that Stuart monarch was not a great patron of music. The invasion of England by Italian singers and musicians did not begin until the end of the century. So, for Corelli, the pursuit of a career meant going either to Venice or Rome. He supposedly did go to Venice for a while, and the once-accepted story that he also went to Paris has been disproved. Marc Pincherle, author of the definitive biography of Corelli, has shown that it was Francesco Cavalli and not Corelli who suffered at the hands of Lully in Paris. Jean-Jacques Rousseau wrote that it was Corelli, but a mistake on his part or on that of a transcriber accounts for the confusion of names.

We do not know for certain when Corelli first appeared in Rome. It may have been in 1671, when he was eighteen, for there is some indirect evidence that he was playing there at a theater, the Tor di Nova, that recently had come under the patronage of the exiled Queen Christina of Sweden, who, having abdicated in 1654, then embraced the Catholic faith and kept a lavish and very musical court in Rome.

The irrefutable evidence places Corelli in Rome in 1675, in which year the records show that he played at the annual festival in the church of Saint-Louis-des-Français, a festival in which he participated as a violinist on and off until 1709. It has been conjectured that in the years for which there are no records of his activities, he was absent from Rome, either at the court of Modena or in Germany at various courts. No evidence has been found for this. Corelli did dedicate works to German princes and to a German princess and his name appears in certain German records, but it now is evident that here again his name was confused with another, in this case with that of Giuseppe Torelli, a notable violinist of the Bolognese school who was one of those who developed the solo concerto.

So far as we can tell, Corelli's chief patron until 1687 appears to have been Queen Christina, for whom in that year he led an orchestra of 150 strings at a gala concert honoring the English ambassador, the Earl of Castelmaine. An allegoric cantata by Alessandro Guidi with additions by Corelli's friend, Bernardo Pasquini, was given on this occasion. Lully's pupil, Georg Muffat, wrote of hearing the concertos of Corelli in 1682 in Christina's Palazzo Riario, where she maintained her collections and an assemblage of poets, musicians, artists, and philosophers that she called the Accademia dei Lincei. Learned societies of various kinds had by this time been established throughout Europe.

Queen Christina died in greatly reduced circumstances in 1689. Two years earlier, Corelli had entered the employ of Cardinal Panfili, for whom he acted as music master and in whose *palazzo* he lived. He remained in the Cardinal's employ for three years, after which he entered into the service of one of the great patrons of the time, Cardinal Ottoboni.

Corelli in 1690 became Cardinal Ottoboni's first violin and director of music, retaining that position for the rest of his life. He took up residence in the Cancelleria, though he maintained another small apartment in the Palazetto Ermini, chiefly to house members of his family. He had three older brothers and an older sister, to whom he was devoted. Since Corelli never married and had never known his father, who died a month before he was born, it is reasonable to assume that he was more than usually dependent upon his brothers and sister, who appear to have benefited, at least indirectly, from the Cardinal's patronage.

The best of Roman society gathered at the Cancelleria to enjoy the Cardinal's lavish hospitality. On Monday nights, he gave musical entertainments that soon were famous far beyond the borders of Italy. The celebrated "contest" between Domenico Scarlatti and George Frederick Handel took place in the Cancelleria in 1709. It must have been at this time that Handel reportedly objected to the way Corelli was playing some of his music and insisted on showing him how it should be done, after which Corelli supposedly said: "But, my dear Saxon, this is in the French style, which I do not understand."

To Corelli, the Cardinal was both patron and friend, and through him he became the leading musician of Rome and celebrated throughout Europe. The luxury and splendor that surrounded him failed to affect him, however, and he remained a quiet but strong man, essentially simple, basically modest but aware of his own worth, unaffected, and frugal almost to the point of parsimoniousness. His life was successful and serene, though he did have flashes of temper. Most importantly, he had security and could compose at his own pace, which, since he was something of a perfectionist, was slow.

One of the romantizations of Corelli's life concerns his appearance with Alessandro Scarlatti's orchestra in Naples, which supposedly resulted in a humiliation so intense that it led to his death of a broken heart. There is no real proof that Corelli ever appeared in Naples, though he may have done. Certainly, he knew Alessandro Scarlatti (father of Domenico), who was a prominent operatic composer and fellow member of the Accademia dei Arcadi, a society of people working in or concerned with the arts that succeeded the academy founded by Queen Christina. It may have been true that Scarlatti could compose passages that would strain Corelli's technical capacities as a violinist and offend his sensibilities as a composer. But if the appearance did take place and was a fiasco, it certainly had no more than a passing effect on Corelli, who had only to return to Rome, where he was loved and never challenged, either as player or composer.

Corelli's career as a public performer ended in 1710. He died on January 8, 1713, in his apartment in the Palazetto Ermini. Cardinal Ottoboni arranged for his burial in the church of Santa Maria della Rotunda, which is the Pantheon, though it had not yet become the burial place of national heroes.

Of the violins that Corelli played and which he bequeathed to Matteo Fornari, nothing is known. One of them may have been the famous Stradivarius known as the "Corelli," which later disappeared completely, and another that supposedly had painted decorations by the artist, Annibale Carracci, probably was a sixteenth-century model by Andrea Amati. Corelli also possessed a violin by the Austrian maker, Matthias Albani.

Of Corelli's musical importance, much has been written and quite a bit argued. Though his chief importance was as the originator of the *concerto grosso* form, which did much in the development of orchestral music, his finest writing for the violin is found in his *Sonate a tre*, sets of which are included in his first five opuses. The *concerti grossi* that are his Opus 6 were posthumously published, though they were much performed by his own orchestra before his death. Of these, the best known today is the beautiful *Christmas Concerto* (actually a concerto for Christmas Eve). Violinists are still partial to Corelli's variations on the Spanish dance, *La Follia*. The only description we have of Corelli as a player mentions grimaces, rolling eyeballs, and other eccentricities. But passion was expected of players in those days. Today, a calm demeanor that conceals all effort is considered desirable and is typical of such great contemporary violinists as Jascha Heifetz and Nathan Milstein. But there are others, also great, who groan, gasp, and twist their faces in the agonized attempt to achieve perfection. One ignores what one sees for the sake of what one hears, though Corelli apparently was admired the more in his day for showing what he felt.

Though the music of Corelli achieved depths not known before in sonority and profundity, he can not be called a pioneer or innovator. His violin technique was limited, more so than that of his contemporaries Torelli, Biber, Walther, and G. B. Vitali. What he did accomplish has been described by Marc Pincherle as supplying "the link between the counterpoint of the seventeenth century and the melodic emancipation of the eighteenth."

The influence of Corelli was profound and lasting. His pupils learned much from him and took what they learned to many places. Among these were some of the greatest violinists of the next generation, particularly Francesco Geminiani, G. B. Somis, and Pietro Locatelli.

After Corelli's death, Cardinal Ottoboni ennobled his family, a fitting tribute to so noble a musician.

4

Antonio Vivaldi

c. 1678–1741

The tourists that today sustain the beautiful but somnolent city of Venice can imagine what it must have been like during its days of glory. The paintings of Francesco Guardi, whose career was beginning as that of Antonio Vivaldi was ending, represent, both in content and meaning, the essence of Venice in the twilight of its greatness. Significantly, the city's long decline in political and economic power coincided with its rise in artistic importance. The austerity of power gave way to the love of luxury, pleasure, diversion, and pageantry, characteristic of the Venetians in the late seventeenth and early eighteenth centuries. Venice was the great carnival city of Europe. Chief among its pleasures was that of music, for the Venetians of that time were passionately musical. Every gondolier was a singer; the common people gathered in the squares and sang spontaneously; ten or more opera houses, each patronized by a noble family, were in operation. All the leading musicians of Europe came there if they could. Of the four geniuses of the baroque era of music, whose works represent the apogee of its style, Vivaldi was a Venetian, Handel and Scarlatti spent protracted periods in

Venice, and J. S. Bach, though he never visited Italy, was
much influenced by Vivaldi.

Vivaldi, like Domenico Scarlatti, is a discovery of the
twentieth century. His music was totally forgotten after his
death, which may seem strange to us today, when it is so
much in fashion. But the entire body of baroque music was
ignored during the classical period that followed. Bach himself remained in obscurity for three-quarters of a century
after his death. Even his sons, who were far better known to
their contemporaries, saw no reason for forcing their father's works upon the public, which was indifferent to the
music of the past and interested only in "novelties." It remained for Felix Mendelssohn, beginning in 1829, to reveal
the wonders of Bach. In the case of Handel, whose position
in England was almost that of a national monument, the
fashion for him faded after his death but was more quickly
revived. Vivaldi, however, hardly existed in the minds of
music lovers until modern times, though his name became
known again during the Bach revival, but only as the obscure composer of violin concertos that the master tran-
scribed for the harpsichord.

Bach, Handel, and Scarlatti, all born in the same year
(1685), were seven or eight years younger than Vivaldi.
Bach's career was entirely in Germany, Handel's mostly in
England, and Scarlatti's mainly in Spain. Though Bach and
Handel composed superb music for the violin, they were
principally keyboard players. Scarlatti was exclusively a
harpsichordist, who, despite his attempts to emulate his father, Alessandro, by composing operas, is important only as
a composer of harpsichord sonatas. Vivaldi, on the other
hand, was first and foremost a violinist, though he, too, zeal-
ously lent himself to the composition of operas, producing
more than forty, the value of which remains unknown to us
today. Opera was the rage in his time; and the money was to
be made composing for the many theaters in Italy that were
always in need of new works. Baroque opera, with its emphasis on mythological subjects, allegory, stage machinery,
and spectacle, was seldom much more than a medium for

singing. Rowdy audiences hardly paid attention to the music except when a famous singer was launched upon an aria, which he or she freely embellished at will. Vivaldi apparently caught the attention when he played a cadenza of his own devising during the course of one of his own operas. If he did not actually originate the cadenza, as has been claimed, he certainly developed it and created a fashion for it.

The static nature of baroque opera has banished it from opera houses, where hardly anything earlier than Gluck and Mozart is in the permanent repertory. Operas of Monteverdi and Handel are frequently revived; and of late, other seventeenth- and early eighteenth-century works have been produced with some success, particularly one or two of the many by Cavalli, the pupil of Monteverdi. Perhaps we will hear something of the Vivaldi operas eventually. Certainly, his oratorio, *Juditha triumphans,* which is almost an opera, contains much beautiful and dramatic music. But it is possible that, as some scholars tell us, the operas of Vivaldi were so quickly and carelessly composed, and so much to formula, that they are essentially uninteresting. Vivaldi himself boasted that he had composed one of his operas in five days; but this is not quite so extraordinary as it sounds, for he wrote down only the melodic line for the singers, leaving its embellishment to them, and merely indicated the harmonic outlines of the accompaniment. He also boasted that he could compose concertos faster than a copyist could copy them. His manuscripts show that he worked out a kind of musical shorthand, which created difficulties for posterity. In one way, Vivaldi was fortunate to remain unknown until modern times. Otherwise, he would have suffered at the hands of editors and arrangers of the classical and romantic periods, who freely adapted the works of composers such as Corelli, Tartini, Veracini, Locatelli, Torelli, and Geminiani to suit their own taste and that of their period. Modern scholarship has restored Vivaldi to us as he was and not as someone thought he should be.

Only a few of Vivaldi's letters and a few contemporary ac-

counts of him are available. From these, and from some secondary accounts, a reasonably accurate account of his life
can be given in outline, thanks to the researches and sound
deductions of modern scholars, particularly Arnold Schering, who early in this century did much to bring about the
Vivaldi revival, and Marc Pincherle, the contemporary
French musicologist, who wrote the definitive study of his
life and works. The English scholar, Arthur Hutchins, has
also made important contributions to the study of Vivaldi
and his works.

There had been important Vivaldis in medieval and Renaissance times—one, in fact, was Doge of Genoa in the mid-
sixteenth century. But whether the composer could claim
descent from them is not known. His father, Giovanni Battista, also a violinist, was employed in the ducal chapel of
the Cathedral of San Marco in Venice, which had enjoyed
the highest reputation for music since the time of Monteverdi. Of the three sons of Giovanni Battista Vivaldi, two
were barbers and the third became a priest. This was the
composer himself, who, because of his red hair, was always
known as "Il Prete rosso," or "the red priest."

Presumably, Vivaldi's teachers were his father and Giovanni Legrenzi, who was *maestro di cappella* of the ducal
chapel from 1685 to his death in 1690 and composed modest
but idiomatic trio sonatas for the violin. It was just at this
time, when Vivaldi was entering his teens, that the first solo
concertos were being composed by Giuseppe Torelli, a violinist of the Bolognese school, who at this time was employed at
the courts of Vienna and Ansbach. Vivaldi's slightly older
contemporary and fellow Venetian, Tommaso Albinioni, a
violinist and opera composer, must have had some influence
upon him in this respect, for some of his solo concertos pre-
date the first by Vivaldi and are in more conventional style.
He shares with Vivaldi the distinction of having had his
music borrowed by Bach.

Much speculation has surrounded the fact that soon after
he became a priest in 1703, Vivaldi ceased to say Mass and
devoted himself exclusively to music. The chief reason for

this appears to have been a physical infirmity, which struck early and persisted for life, making it difficult for him to walk unaided and necessitated his traveling always with a retinue of four or five persons. Then, too, the times were lax, and it is doubtful whether anyone thought there was anything wrong, or even unusual, about a priest who served God entirely through music. Perhaps there were some who were shocked at the thought of a priest composing for and performing in theaters. If there was any disapproval from the Church itself, there is no record of it, nor is there any reason to believe that Vivaldi was not true to his vows. He remained strictly devout throughout his life and, apparently, was as conscious of himself as a priest as he was of himself as a musician.

One of the extraordinary institutions of the time in Venice, which also existed in Naples, were the *ospedali* or *conservatori*. These had begun as asylums for orphans and at first were merely shelters supported by the city. But as the power and popularity of music increased, they became training schools for musicians, at first only partially but finally almost exclusively. Since there was such a demand for music and no member of the aristocracy, no matter how talented, would become a public performer, the *ospedali* became the centers, along with the music chapels of the churches, of all non-theatrical musical activity. They were the forerunners of the great European secular conservatories of the nineteenth century. In Venice, the *ospedali* were exclusively for girls; and in Vivaldi's time, the singers and instrumentalists trained in them were so celebrated that the public flocked to their concerts. Some of the girls were accomplished violinists who enjoyed great fame locally (the most famous, Regina Strinasacchi, belonged to a later era). Only a few of the *ospedali* orphans took religious vows, though they were supervised by nuns and concealed from the public behind iron grills or screens; and some of them, not withstanding their lack of social background, made advantageous marriages.

Many of Vivaldi's instrumental works were composed for performance by the girls of the Ospedale (or Ospitale in the

Venetian dialect) della Pietà, where he was *maestro de' concerti* and *maestro di coro* for thirty-seven years, beginning in 1703. He made it the most famous of the *ospedali* in Venice. The others—the Incurabili, the Mendicanti, and the Santi Giovanni e Paolo—went out of existence before the end of the eighteenth century. But the Pietà persisted, though but feebly, until it was replaced by a modern conservatory in 1877.

Though Vivaldi was officially connected with the Pietà, which was his base of operations and, so to speak, his bread-and-butter job, he was always involved in the productions of his operas, both in Venice at one or another of the many theaters, or in other Italian cities, including Ferrara, Ancona, Mantua, Vicenza, Milan, Verona, and Rome. During his lifetime, there were also productions of his operas in Vienna and Munich. We do not have records of exactly where and when Vivaldi traveled, though it has been established that he died and was buried in a pauper's grave in Vienna, not Venice, in July of 1741. It is also almost certain that he visited Amsterdam, where his music was published. His dedications to the Landgrave (or Duke) of Hesse-Darmstadt led historians to suppose that Vivaldi spent some time in Germany in his service, though actually the Landgrave was governor at Mantua during the years (1720–23) when Vivaldi could have served him.

What we know of Vivaldi as a violinist comes to us from a description left by a musical amateur and friend of the composer, Johann Friedrich Uffenbach of Frankfort. He wrote, after hearing Vivaldi play at a performance of one of his operas in 1715: "Vivaldi performed a solo accompaniment admirably, and at the end he added an improvised cadenza that quite confounded me, for such playing has not been heard before and can never be equalled. He placed his fingers but a hair's breadth from the bridge so that there was hardly room for the bow. He played thus on all four strings, with imitations and at unbelievable speed. . . . I cannot say that it captivated me, because it was more skillfully executed than it was pleasant to hear." Later, Uffenbach ordered ten *concerti grossi* from Vivaldi, which were delivered in three days' time. Uffenbach went on record as doubting whether they were composed expressly for him, as Vivaldi claimed.

Vivaldi's most important pupil was Johann Georg Pisendel, a protégé of the Elector of Saxony, who studied with him in 1717. Pisendel later had many contacts with Bach and provides a link between him and Vivaldi. Bach may have learned much about violin technique from Pisendel and therefore indirectly from Vivaldi. The mystery of how the great Bach sonatas and partitas for solo violin actually were played in his time never has been solved, for violinists today can not, for instance, play the chords as written but must arpeggiate them. Some scholars even went so far as to invent a very rounded bow, claiming it was the authentic Bach bow; but other, more temperate scholars have discredited it as being impractical in all respects except the playing of chords.

Though Vivaldi died in poverty and was promptly forgotten, he enjoyed considerable renown in his lifetime. His published music was admired beyond Italy (it had a great vogue in France) and had much influence on his contemporaries, beginning with the famous *L'Estro armonico,* op. 3, published about 1712 but much circulated in manuscript copies before that. These concertos, together with the *La Stravaganza,* op. 4 and the *Il Cimento,* op. 9, which includes the now celebrated *Four Seasons,* and many others, constitute Vivaldi's large body of concertos. They are his finest work, though some of his church music, particularly the splendid *Gloria,* ranks with them.

The music reflects the times as well as the man. For both were concerned with description and theatrical effect, with the liveliness of dance combined with a kind of elevated pathos suitable to mythological or historical personages. Vivaldi was the first to transfer to his instrumental *adagios* the kind of sustained slow melody typical of the moments of sublime pathos in baroque opera. It is not the free, varied melody that was to come later. Still, in the best of the con-

certos, the combination of driving rhythms and sustained
lyricism is enchanting. The concertos, as least in their outer
movements, adhere to the pattern of alternating *tuttis* and
solos (usually *tutti-*solo*-tutti-*solo*-tutti*). The solos merely
elaborate on the thematic material announced in the *tuttis*.
In these concertos, the vitality of the music is often astound-
ing, particularly considering the long years that they lay dor-
mant.

Since he worked at high speed and indefatigably, Vivaldi
was forced to borrow from himself and sometimes—as was
the accepted custom of his day—from others. It is a wonder
that so many of his works are as nearly perfect as they are.
In all, he composed more than four hundred concertos,
about half of which are for one or more violins and the rest
for various combinations of other string instruments, including mandolins, or wind instruments. It has been claimed for
Vivaldi that he was the first to compose for the clarinet. He
also was one of the creators of program music and pioneered
in composing passages in which the violin imitates not only
birds and effects in nature but other instruments as well,
such as the trumpet.

Vivaldi was fortunate to have been a Venetian, just as the
Venetians were fortunate that he was one of them. Since the
city was wealthy and music there was available to all and
not merely to a few, he could work freely, occupy an important post without being a slave to it, and remain free of the
domination of a single prince or bishop. Many of his contemporaries were not so fortunate.

Bach and Handel, the two gods of the baroque, have now
been joined by Vivaldi, a man who was in many ways, both
temperamentally and artistically, a combination of them.
What Handel learned from Vivaldi—possibly at first hand—
was probably not the same that Bach learned. Handel was a
man of the theater and carried baroque opera to its zenith.
Bach, on the other hand, had more in common with Vivaldi
the priest, though it was his profoundly Protestant nature
that transformed the very Italian violin concertos of Vivaldi
into Germanic keyboard concertos. Was the violin still

looked down upon in Weimar? If so, then Bach must have composed his mighty solo sonatas and partitas and other works for the violin in deference to the Italian school of Vivaldi, Corelli, and Tartini, setting these works apart from the main body of his vast output, which, developing from the laws set down by Schütz, Scheide, Swelinck, Buxtehude, and Pachelbel, was most directly influenced by the organ and strongly and profoundly Germanic.

Yet music transcends nationality, language, race, and religion. However much Bach and Handel discovered in Vivaldi and took from him, they recognized him as an equal, something it took history almost two centuries to do.

5

Francesco Maria Veracini

c. 1690–c. 1750

The term baroque as applied to an era has more artistic than political or economic implications. But the most obvious explanation for the baroque expression, which indicated a new state of mind in Catholic Europe, is the relaxation of the Inquisition and the fanatical censorship of morals and manners that was part of its effect. The Council of Trent (1545–64) established the Counter-Reformation, which corrected some of the abuses of the Church and liberalized some of its thinking, though religious wars went on. The Edict of Nantes, issued in France by Henri IV in 1598, granted tolerance to the Huguenots; but this was revoked in 1685 by Louis XIV, who succeeded in driving them from France.

The baroque style appeared first in literature in the sixteenth century, manifesting itself in the poetic forms known in Spain as Gongorism, in Italy as Marinism, and in English prose as euphuism and later as cultism. In the seventeenth century, the baroque, with its emphasis on decoration and technical virtuosity within a limited scope, developed rapidly in architecture, painting, and sculpture. The simplest definition of the baroque in architecture has been given as "the

avoidance of straight lines at all costs." Baroque churches
and palaces were built in profusion throughout Spain, Portu-
gal, Italy, Austria, Germany, Bohemia, Poland, and, to a
much more limited extent, in France, while in England, the
Palladian style, derived from the great sixteenth-century
architect of Vicenza, Andrea Palladio, became the rage during the seventeenth and eighteenth centuries.

In painting, the baroque began after the death of Michelangelo in 1564. It was best exemplified in the paintings of
Michelangelo Amerighi da Caravaggio, who founded what
was called the naturalist school. He was the master of
chiaroscuro, or the dramatic contrast of light and shade.
During the eighteenth century, travelers on the grand tour
flocked to see the paintings of baroque artists like Caravaggio and his rival, Guido Reni, and remained indifferent to
the medieval and Renaissance masters. Today, museums
that feature baroque pictures are seldom if ever crowded. A
revival of interest may soon take place, however, as already
has happened in music. Thanks to radio and recordings, as
well as to the now advanced science of musicology, baroque
music, so long neglected, has become the fashion.

The Merriam-Webster dictionary defines baroque as applied to music as "a style of composition abounding in the
extreme or irregular, both in harmony and rhythmic organization." Since music, so to speak, was a late bloomer in the
arts, the significance of the baroque in music is not the same
as in architecture, painting, and sculpture, for which it rep-
resents the zenith of technical virtuosity. Musicians of the
baroque era were just beginning to discover the technical
range of their instruments. Symphonic music such as we
know it did not yet exist. Truly dramatic opera was still in its
infancy. The orchestra, by our standards, was a simple
affair. The pianoforte, so much more extended and powerful
than the clavichord or harpsichord and so different in sound,
was not invented until 1711 and not in general use until the
end of the eighteenth century. In fact, the profession of
music was a limited one until the eighteenth century, when
public concerts available to all created new opportunities

and greater freedom for musicians; and it was not until the nineteenth century, when the middle class rather than the aristocracy became its chief supporters, that the almost limitless possibilities of music, both technical and intellectual, were recognized. It was only then that music ceased to be one of the privileges of the privileged, except, of course, in churches, where it was available to all. Strangely, it was at the time when the musical art was reaching maturity that the Church, believing it had become decadent, severely restricted its use in the churches.

If, then, the baroque era was the adolescence of the violin, technically if not musically, it does not mean that its masters were merely precocious. Without Corelli, Vivaldi, and—in the next generation—Veracini, Geminiani, Locatelli, Tartini, and Leclair, there could never have been a Paganini. Of these, and the other masters of the period, the one who apparently came closest to predicting Paganini, both in personality and as an artist, was Francesco Maria Veracini.

He began life with a great advantage, for his uncle and teacher, Antonio Veracini, was a distinguished violinist in the service of Ferdinand II de Médicis, Grand Duke of Tuscany, at his court in Florence. The records are unclear and maddeningly incomplete so far as both the Veracinis are concerned. In both cases, the dates for birth and death are uncertain. It hardly seems possible that, as some sources state, the uncle died in 1696, six years after the nephew was born. Perhaps he died later, or the younger Veracini was born not in 1690 but in 1685, the date given in other sources. Whenever it was, the event took place in Florence, and Francesco Maria Veracini was ever afterwards known as "Il Fiorentino." Antonio Veracini is of some importance in the development of the violin sonata, for he composed many, both *da chiesa* and *da camera*, that, though they are strictly traditional, are not without interest.

The sonata began as several dance forms grouped together and derived from the polyphonic *canzona*. The *sonata da chiesa* was the first to develop movements, generally four or five, that were purely instrumental and, for obvious reasons, not based on dance rhythms. The *sonata da tre*, which preceded the solo sonata, was for three voice parts: two solo players and figured bass, or *basso continuo*. The three-part construction of the sonata, from which the symphonic form evolved and to which the fourth part or *scherzo* movement later was added, was not characteristic in Corelli's time, though it was developed then, and it did not actually become fixed until after Veracini's time. He himself wrote in a preface to his *Sonate Accademiche*, op. 2, published in 1744, that while he had provided four or five movements to each sonata, the player could select three to make up his own sonata. What we call sonata form, which was applied to the symphony and refers strictly to the opening movement—exposition, development, recapitulation—was not established until the mid-eighteenth century.

The ascendency of the homophonic style over the polyphonic came about in the baroque era and led to much uncertainty as well as experimentation. Composers were either cautious or bold; but each generation contributed importantly to the evolution of the forms and tonality that became standard by the end of the eighteenth century and have persisted—with variations—ever since, at least until recent years, when atonality and serialism have more or less taken over.

Veracini was, if born in 1685 instead of 1690, the exact contemporary of Bach, Handel, and Scarlatti and may have died in the same year as Bach. His importance is not as a composer, but as a violin virtuoso. He has been called, and indeed may have been, the first international virtuoso, which means that he gained fame in several countries and, being of a restless nature, did not, as most musicians did in his day, attach himself permanently to a court or chapel. He appeared upon the scene just at the time when it became possible, though only barely, for a musician to make a living at public concerts and not be entirely dependent on princely patrons. However, in Veracini's time, this was true only in London.

Antonio Veracini was his nephew's first teacher. Whether

or not, after his uncle's death, Veracini studied in Rome with Corelli can not be said for certain. Though he proclaimed his allegiance to Corelli, he is not listed as one of his pupils in the biography of Corelli by Marc Pincherle. Other historians say he was a Corelli pupil, though on scant evidence. In fact, almost nothing is known of Veracini's life before 1713, when he appeared in Venice and met Vivaldi. He apparently was by this time a celebrated violinist. In the same year, he made his first trip to London, where he made his debut at the Italian Opera as leader or first violinist. This was at the King's Theatre. Dr. Charles Burney, the music historian, later wrote that Veracini was then "the greatest violinist in Europe," though he himself was not yet born and did not actually hear Veracini play until thirty years later. At the Italian Opera, Veracini performed interludes or "symphonies," as they then were called. Many of the operas in which he played were by Handel; and Dr. Burney later recorded that in ensemble passages, Veracini's strong, firm tone sounded distinctly through and above the rest of the string section. On March 14, 1714, Veracini appeared at a public concert with the mysterious singer known only as "the Baroness." On April 22, he played at his own benefit concert in the hall known as Hickford's Rooms. Other artists appeared with him, as was then the invariable custom. Musicians performed at a colleague's benefit in exchange for his performing at theirs. That way, they all made money eventually.

Public concerts had come into being in London at the end of the seventeenth century. They originated in 1672 with a violinist named John Banister, who got the idea of charging admission to concerts in his own house and advertising them in the newspapers. These were continued by Thomas Britton, who was known as "the musical small-coal man." The first music society, the Academy of Antient Music, which held meetings in taverns, was founded in 1710. Hickford's Rooms in St. James Street, London's first real concert hall, was opened in 1713, the year before Veracini first performed there.

If Veracini had remained in London, he might have had a

much more stable and profitable career. Italian musicians, especially singers, had become the rage there. Handel had been king of the Italian Opera since 1711. Ironically, one of Veracini's most important contemporaries, Francesco Geminiani, a pupil of Corelli, arrived in London in the same year, to remain for the rest of his life. Although he appeared in concerts, performing his own sonatas and *concerti grossi*, he worked mainly as a teacher, composer, and theorist in London and in Dublin, where he died in 1762 at the age of seventy-six, allegedly of a broken heart because the manuscript of one of his treatises had been stolen. His *Art of Playing the Violin,* written in English and published in 1751, is the first treatise for professional violinists.

A story about Geminiani is that he was responsible for reconciling Handel with King George I, who had not forgiven Handel for leaving his employ in Hanover before he became the English king. Geminiani was commanded to perform before the King in 1715 but refused to do so unless Handel accompanied him. The King agreed, and so was reconciled with Handel.

Before going to England, Geminiani had played in the opera orchestra in Naples, where he was engaged as leader but was not permitted to lead because the players could not follow his *tempo rubato.* So passionate and mercurial was his nature, that his contemporary, Giuseppe Tartini, dubbed him "Il furibondo Geminiani." He was a purist and disliked overelaborate ornamentation so much that he often wrote *come sta* over passages in his music that he wanted played as written and without ornamentation. His music remains to this day almost unknown, though some of it has been recorded.

It is not known exactly when Veracini left London, though we do know that he reappeared in Italy in 1716, in which year he was invited to play a "contest" with Giuseppe Tartini in the Palazzo Pisano-Mocenigo in Venice during festivities given in honor of the visiting Elector of Saxony. However, Tartini prudently went ahead of time to hear Veracini play at Cremona and was so impressed (and depressed) that he withdrew from the contest and went into a long retreat. Veracini appeared alone before the Elector of Saxony, who engaged him as one of his court musicians at Dresden. Sources differ as to when Veracini actually went there. Some say it was in 1717 and others 1720. We do know that he remained at Dresden until 1723. It was not a happy time for him, it seems, for according to the gossip of the times, he was unpopular with his fellow musicians at court, who considered him vain and arrogant.

The most famous episode in Veracini's life occurred at Dresden when he hurled himself out of a high window and was lamed for life. It was suggested at the time that he did this because of the humiliation that resulted from a plot against him concocted by his rival, the German violinist Johann Georg Pisendel, Vivaldi's pupil, who was also a court musician to the Elector. Pisendel supposedly had Veracini play a difficult work at sight in the presence of the court and then had it played by a lesser musician, who, because he had secretly studied it thoroughly, was adjudged superior. Another explanation, unsupported by the record, was that Veracini had fits of insanity. Or he may merely have been suffering from a particularly bad case of *chagrin d'amour*.

Veracini left Dresden for Prague, where he entered the service of Count Kinsky, who maintained a very musical court. How long he remained there is unclear, though he undoubtedly met and worked with Tartini, who also was part of Count Kinsky's court at this time. Perhaps the entire twelve-year gap in the record can be filled by assuming that Veracini stayed at Prague until 1735, the year in which he reappeared in London.

Twenty years had brought about many changes in the London musical scene. Handel had gone into eclipse as an opera composer but was re-establishing himself with his oratorios. The success of the English ballad opera, *The Beggar's Opera*, in 1728 had created a new fashion. Still, the Italian Opera continued. Veracini, having found himself overshadowed by Geminiani, decided to try his hand at opera. His

Ariadne was produced at the King's Theatre on November 25, 1735, and was an enormous success, being repeated seventeen times. The cast contained four of the greatest singers not only of that time but of all time, the *castrati* Farinelli and Senesino, the soprano Francesca Cuzzoni, and the contralto Francesca Bertolli.

The record indicates that Veracini stayed in London for ten years. He produced four more operas there. He also composed cantatas and many sonatas, including the *Sonate Accademiche,* which appeared in 1744 and were dedicated to the Elector Augustus III of Saxony, perhaps in the hope that he would be invited back to Dresden. These sonatas contain some of the first specific signs to indicate nuances, particularly *crescendo* and *diminuendo.* The Veracini violin concertos are conventional, but the sonatas continued the advance in the form, the earlier ones being composed in the traditional dance forms, while the later ones are made up of movements in the more advanced, abstract forms, such as *allegro, adagio,* etc.

After Dr. Burney heard Veracini play in a London concert in 1745, he described his style as "bold." That a young man could say this about the playing of an old man is interesting and indicates that Veracini's power and skill must have been extraordinary for those times. The picture of him that is printed as the frontispiece for his *Sonate Accademiche* shows him playing with the violin against the collarbone instead of gripped by the chin. This was probably how he held his instrument, though it is just possible that he held it that way only part of the time, particularly when posing for his portrait. Another portrait of a violinist done six years earlier clearly indicates that the player held his instrument at the neck.

Whatever happened to Veracini after 1745 remains a mystery. He apparently left England in that year; and it was believed that he perished in a shipwreck on his way back to Italy, together with the two Stainer violins that were his constant companions and which he called Peter and Paul, after the saints. It is now believed that if indeed he was in the shipwreck, he survived it. More likely, he was not in it at all and returned to Italy overland or on a different ship. There is now some evidence that he settled near Pisa, where he lived in greatly reduced circumstances at least until 1750, the year of Bach's death.

6

Giuseppe Tartini

1692–1770

Slow to develop and a modest, retiring man, Giuseppe Tartini was in many ways the opposite of his celebrated rival, F. M. Veracini, who, though much admired as a player, was disliked as a person. By the time he died at seventy-seven, Tartini had become one of the most revered musicians in Europe and was much loved by everybody who knew him. Though his early life was romantic and has been much romanticized, he was, in fact—at least in maturity—a stable, industrious person, a domestic man who hated to travel and was content to let the world come to him, which, in the end, it did.

Of the great violinists who came immediately after Corelli and Vivaldi, three—Geminiani, Locatelli, and Somis—were actually pupils of Corelli, and Veracini might have been. G. B. Somis, who became a great teacher and lived to be ninety-six, also had direct contact with and possibly had lessons from Vivaldi, though they were the same age. Tartini, on the other hand, appears to have been largely self-taught. He himself said that he did not study the violin seriously until he was past thirty, which must have been an overly

modest statement, since his playing had become celebrated
long before he reached that age.

Born at Pirano in Istria—now part of Yugoslavia—on
April 8, 1692, Tartini came from a family that originally
was Florentine. Three brothers and a sister died in infancy.
His father was a wealthy man who eventually was ennobled;
he also was extremely devout and bent every effort to per-
suade the young Tartini to become a monk of the Minori
Conventuali. Tartini resisted, however, and, after studies at
the Collegio dei Padri delle Scuole Pie at Capo d'Istria, near
Pirano, was sent to the University of Padua to study law. His
success at the University was not as a law student but as a
fencer. In fact, he seriously considered opening a fencing
school at Naples as a means of supporting himself while
studying music. No doubt he had had some training in
music at Pirano and probably took further lessons at Padua.
He may also have given lessons, for the girl with whom he
fell in love in 1713, Elisabetta Premazone, was said to have
been his pupil. She was the ward of a powerful man, Giorgio
Cardinal Cornaro, who, after she and Tartini were secretly
married, was so enraged that he ordered the bridegroom's
arrest. Tartini's family also were enraged and cut him off
financially. Tartini was forced to flee, leaving his bride behind at Padua. Disguising himself as a monk, he wandered
southwards for some time, finally taking refuge in the monastery of Saint Francis at Assisi, where he remained for
about two years.

As it turned out, Tartini's enforced exile was good fortune
in disguise, for he was sympathetically received at Assisi and
may even have come under the influence of some musical
monk of the monastery. At any rate, he studied hard and
made certain important discoveries. He experimented with
thicker strings and developed an overhand bow that was
lighter than the ones then in use. His acoustical experiments
led to his discovery of the *terzi tuoni*, which are differential
or combination tones. This development, so important to violin playing, was also credited to a German theorist, Georg
Andreas Sorge, who may have discovered the third tones in-

dependently but at a later date, for he was only about twelve years old at this time.

Tartini also began to play at services in the monastery and soon attracted crowds, although he remained unseen, carefully concealed behind a curtain or screen. At this time he composed what is still his most famous work, the sonata that he called *Il Trillo del Diavolo*. The "Devil's Trill" of the title is the *trillo accompagnato,* a trill accompanied by another part and incorporating double stops and extensions. This sonata became one of the great showpieces for virtuosos and even today appears on recital programs, usually as the "warm-up" piece. According to the account of the French astronomer, Joseph de Lalande, who years later had it from Tartini himself, the sonata was composed very quickly after Tartini had a dream in which he made a pact with the Devil, who, taking up Tartini's violin, played a marvelous sonata, so marvelous, in fact, that Tartini said his *Devil's Trill* Sonata was but a poor approximation of it.

According to legend, Tartini's exile ended as the result of his identity being discovered accidentally when the curtain behind which he was playing was inadvertently pulled back. This was on the day of the Saint Francis pilgrimage, August 1, 1715, and some Paduans, who immediately recognized Tartini, were present. Apparently they praised his playing in such glowing terms when they returned to Padua, that Cardinal Cornaro relented and called Tartini back. The marriage was finally sanctioned, and the young couple were reunited.

It was in the following year, 1716, that Tartini, whose fame had spread, was invited to compete against Veracini at Venice, and having journeyed first to Cremona to hear "Il Fiorentino," thought better of the proposed contest and decided to renege. Whether in fear of reprisals or simply from the realization of his own limitations as a player compared to Veracini, he then went into a long retreat at Ancona.

For the next five years, Tartini stayed in obscurity, studying and working. During this period, he had lessons from the man he credited with being his first, and perhaps only, teacher, one Giulio Terni, about whom little or nothing is known. Perhaps he helped Tartini with his bowing, in which he had found Veracini particularly superior.

In 1721, when he was still twenty-nine and not yet thirty, the age at which he said he really began to study the violin, Tartini became the solo violinist at the Capella del Santo in Padua, which was celebrated for its music. Here his playing attracted much attention and admiration. Two years later, he went to the court of Count Kinsky at Prague, where he was greatly successful. His stay in Prague, which lasted three years, was his only time outside Italy, though throughout his life he received constant and lucrative offers from London and Paris, where he had a big reputation. Though he hated to leave Padua and did so reluctantly, he did appear at various times—always to great ovations—in Venice, Florence, Leghorn, Bologna, and Palermo. In Naples, he was much embarrassed by the attempt of a crowd to lift him on their shoulders and carry him through the streets like a conquering hero. His performing career was crowned by an appearance in Rome before Pope Clement XII, who commissioned from him the *Miserere* that was sung in the Sistine Chapel on the following Ash Wednesday.

Unfortunately, not much is known about Tartini's three years in Prague or about his relations with Veracini, who was also at Count Kinsky's court at the time. About the only specific fact that we have for this period in Tartini's life is that he played at the coronation of the Holy Roman Emperor, Charles VI, as King of Bohemia.

It may have been that when he returned to Padua in 1726, Tartini already had decided upon his course and for that reason had given up his position at Prague, though it has been suggested that discontent on the part of his wife was the most influential factor. The record is not clear about when he founded his "School of Nations" at Padua. It may have been in the year of his return or perhaps not until two years later. The "Master of Nations," as Tartini was called, received pupils from all over Europe for the next forty years. Though he worked hard at teaching and on various aspects of violin technique, he found time to compose, producing many concertos and sonatas. His concertos represent the strongest link between the earlier works in the form by Vivaldi and later ones by Viotti and Mozart.

Tartini was pious, fond of painting, and of a literary bent, as attested by his use of quotations from Petrarch on his scores. One of his best-known sonatas, the tenth, is titled *Didone abandonnata*, after Vergil. In composing sonatas, he sometimes departed from the then-established fast-slow-fast form and used the unusual form of slow-fast-faster. He also composed concertos for cello and flute. His *L'Arte del Arco* (The Art of Bowing), published in 1758, consists of thirty-eight (later expanded to fifty) variations on a theme by Corelli, whose work he much revered. This kind of musical exercise was not yet common, though it had precedents in such works as Corelli's *La Follia* variations (1700) and the earlier and less-well-known fifty variations of Johann Jakob Walther in his *Hortulus Chelicus* (1688).

Tartini's only real treatise is one on ornaments, with which he was much concerned. The *Traité des Agrémens* was not actually published (and in French) until the year after his death, 1771, though copies of the manuscript must have been widely circulated, since Leopold Mozart used parts of it in his *Violinschule* of 1756.

Though we are familiar with some of Tartini's music, a good deal of it has remained unknown and in manuscript. He was definitely a transitional figure in that his music is of the baroque but in some ways looks forward to the classical period. He was particularly interested in expanding the cadenza and developed it into the *capriccio*, which left nothing to improvisation and extended to as much as fifty measures in his concertos. As for his violin technique, which must in most respects have developed beyond that of any of his contemporaries except Locatelli, all we know of it, apart from what can be deduced from his compositions, is found in a long letter he wrote to one of his pupils, Maddalena Lombardini, who as Madame Sirmen later was much admired for her playing in Paris and London. From it we can learn something of Tartini's attitudes toward rapid and slow *vibrato* (produced with finger and wrist rather than the entire arm), *messa da voce,* mordents, *appoggiatura,* octave leaps, etc. By the time of this letter of Tartini's, violin technique, even more in Locatelli's hands than his, had reached a degree of difficulty and complexity far beyond that known to Corelli and Vivaldi. Sonority had gained from increased extensions; double, triple, and quadruple stops (characteristic in the Bach sonatas) were called for; and semitones in the chromatic scale could be played without sliding from one to the other (as Geminiani specifies in his scores).

Pietro Locatelli, who was born at Bergamo on September 3, 1695, was, with Veracini, Geminiani, and Leclair, the most important of Tartini's contemporaries. A pupil of Corelli while still very young, he appears to have wandered for some time before settling in Amsterdam, where he dominated musical life for many years until his death in 1764. He wrote many concertos and sonatas, some of them important in the development of those forms, and, like Tartini, developed the cadenza into the *capriccio.* Some of his caprices are overextended to the point where they could hardly have been played, from which it can be deduced that he anticipated the ultimate capacities of his instrument but could not reproduce them. His caprices in the concertos published as *L'Arte del violino* (1733) cover the entire range of the violin in that period and indicate a technical virtuosity that extended to the use of the fourteenth position, though only on the E string. Since the fourth position was the highest in common use in those times, Locatelli's extraordinary technical demands may have been for him more theoretical than practical.

Tartini remained active until 1768, when his health began to fail. He was visited in Padua by many of the great men of his time. Unfortunately, no one appears to have cared much for his wife, to whom, however, he remained completely devoted. Not much is known about her, except that she was of a nervous temperament. Whatever her faults, Tartini was either unaware of them or able to overlook them.

The best-known and favorite pupil of Tartini, Pietro Nardini, came to stay with his master while he was dying. Though already famous and much in demand, he remained with Tartini until the end, which came on February 26, 1770.

Nardini, who was born in 1722 and died in 1793, had been violinist at the ducal court in Stuttgart for fifteen years before Tartini's final illness and death. Afterwards, he became director of music for the Grand Duke of Tuscany in Florence. Leopold Mozart described his playing as beautifully expressive but without technical feats. He composed sonatas and concertos, using the full sonata form at the end of his life. According to contemporary accounts, he played so feelingly that his listeners wept; and he wept, too, spilling tears over his violin as he played.

A very modern tribute to the illustrious "Master of Nations" is contained in an orchestral work by the contemporary Italian composer, Luigi Dallapiccola, an avant-garde version of the baroque called *Tartiniana.*

7

Jean-Marie Leclair

1697–1764

In France, where Louis XIV, the "Grand Monarch," reigned for seventy-two years, the musical tradition established by Lully, the king's favorite, remained in force for fifty years after his death. Ballet divertissements stayed the fashion, with the necessary accompaniment of religious music. The twenty-four *violons du roy* enjoyed continuous life, playing mostly for dancing. The viols and lutes were still preferred over the violin for "serious" music; and the advances in violin technique and the violin sonata brought about in Italy were either ignored or resisted. The Musicians' Guild and the official court violinists were strongly reactionary, opposed to all change and suspicious of foreign influences. However, certain French violinists, contemporary with Vivaldi and generally Italian-trained, composed sonatas and contributed somewhat to the evolution of the French school, which, in the course of a century, slowly absorbed the Italian influence, gradually developed its own characteristics, and eventually became pre-eminent. Some of these early violinists and *sonatistes* were Jean-Baptiste Anet, a pupil of Corelli, who, since he lived to be more than ninety, followed the development of his instrument over three generations; his pupil, Jean-Baptiste Senaillé, a court violinist; Elisabeth-Claude Jacquet de la Guerre, who composed harpsichord sonatas with optional violin parts; J. F. Rebel, an opera composer and impresario; and François Duval, who first performed the sonatas of Corelli in France. These were the immediate predecessors of Jean-Marie Leclair, the man who, more than any other, established the French school of violin playing and composed the first characteristically French sonatas and concertos.

The first of eight children of Antoine Leclair of Lyons, a master lace maker and amateur musician, Jean-Marie Leclair was known as Leclair *l'aîné* to distinguish him from a younger brother who bore the same name and was known as Leclair *le cadet*. Four of Leclair's brothers and one of his sisters became professional musicians. Leclair *l'aîné* began his career as a dancer and may have appeared first at a theater in Rouen. In 1716, at the age of nineteen, he married a singer, Marie-Rose Castagné. His first book of violin sonatas was published in 1722, the year in which he became ballet master at the Piedmontese court in Turin. We do not know what events led to this appointment, nor do we know much about what he did in Turin, apart from the fact that he choreographed several ballet sequences for the court entertainments.

Though Leclair remained in Turin only for a year, he was so much affected by his meeting with and lessons from the great Italian violinist and teacher, Giovanni Battista Somis, a pupil of Corelli, that it changed the course of his life. After arriving in Paris in 1723, he secured the patronage of a wealthy bourgeois named Bonnier, to whom he dedicated his second book of sonatas. Three years later, this patronage made it possible for him to return to Turin for a period of intense study with Somis.

With his brother, Lorenzo, also a violinist and composer, G. B. Somis, a native of Piedmont, was the dominant musical influence in Turin. He was court conductor and solo violinist to the Duke of Savoy, who at this time had also become

King of Sardinia. Thirty years older than Leclair, Somis lived to be ninety-six and served through several reigns at the Piedmontese court. Leclair outlived him by only one year. Through him, Leclair became the link between the Italian school of Corelli, Vivaldi, and their successors and the French school that, by the end of the century, was to become dominant.

In 1728, Leclair returned to Paris. M. Bonnier had died, but his son continued as Leclair's patron. The new French King, Louis XV, who had succeeded in 1715, was at this time only eighteen, too young to bring about changes, at least in the musical establishment. One significant change had taken place, however, three years before, when a member of the court band, Anne Danican Philidor, one of a large family of musicians, founded the *Concert spirituel*, the first public concerts in France. These were at first given over entirely to religious music and took place only during the Lenten season, when the Opéra and other theaters were closed. By the time Leclair returned to Paris, instrumental music was beginning to appear on the programs. He must have been one of the first to appear at these concerts as a solo violinist and performed at them regularly until 1736. During these years, he studied composition with André Charon, to whom he dedicated his first book of concertos. In 1734–35, he was a member of the orchestra at the Opéra. Opposition to him from his fellow musicians was strong, for they were cliquish, suspicious, and intolerant of rivals. Finally, in 1736, the conflict came to a head when Leclair openly quarreled with the violinist Jean Pierre Guignon, who had the favor of the King.

Guignon, a native of Turin, was five years younger than Leclair and was also a student of Somis. He and Leclair had performed together at the *Concert spirituel* and at one concert, on Christmas Day, 1734, played in what became a "contest" between them, thus creating some excitement and controversy. Guignon's playing, apparently, was fiery and colorful, while Leclair's was pure and impeccable. When, after the concert, which the King had attended, the two men were appointed to serve alternately—a month at a time—as solo violinists of the royal chapel, Guignon deferred to Leclair, permitting him to serve first. But this arrangement lasted only two years and ended when the two violinists quarreled. Leclair, who seems to have had a strange and difficult character, retired to private life. Guignon, on the other hand, was given a monopoly by the King and the obsolete title of *roi des ménétriers*. He was to be the last musician of the French court to be known as "the king of the violins." Surviving Leclair by ten years, he left some interesting sonatas that show his rival's influence and contain some technical advancements beyond those incorporated by Leclair.

The period of the regency that followed the death of Louis XIV in 1715 and lasted under two regents, the Duc d'Orléans and the Duc de Bourbon, until 1726, when Cardinal Fleury became the power behind the throne, was one of cynicism and decadence. Louis XIV, "the Sun King," had ruled absolutely, keeping the nobles comfortably but carefully in check at Versailles. His ministers and generals were of the bourgeoisie; and it was the bourgeoisie that profited most from his reign, which was the classical period for France, producing in literature such immortals as Molière, Racine, Corneille, Pascal, and La Fontaine. Though Leclair did not live into the period known as "the age of enlightenment," it had its beginnings in his time. The "enlightened despots" of the second half of the eighteenth century had their predecessors in the first half, particularly Louis XV of France, the Sun King's grandson, and Peter the Great of Russia, who died in 1725. Louis XV, unlike the Russian Czar, was very much a *laissez-faire* monarch ruled by his ministers and mistresses. But France still set the style. Elegance was all; and the common people paid for it with heavy taxation. The bourgeois assaults on absolutism and its abuses, already implicit in the comedies of Molière, soon were to come out in the open. The great voices of "the enlightenment," those of Voltaire, Rousseau, and Diderot, were beginning to be heard in the last years of Leclair's life. Frederick the Great of Prussia, a great music patron, mounted his throne in 1740, twenty-four years before Leclair's death, while Catherine the Great seized power in Russia just two years earlier. Perhaps the writer who best expressed the spirit of the exact period in which Leclair lived in Paris was the playwright and novelist, Pierre Marivaux, whose elegant and rueful comedies, like the exquisite but wistful paintings of another contemporary, Antoine Watteau, could most perfectly be accompanied by the music of Leclair.

For seven years after retiring from his court position, Leclair maintained himself by teaching and composing. His first wife died, and he was married again, in 1730, to Louise Roussel, a widow of thirty who was an expert engraver and did much of the work in printing his music. That Leclair's reputation had spread abroad rapidly we know from an article about him that was included in a musical dictionary by J. C. Walther published in Leipzig in 1732. However, we do not know exactly when Leclair went to Holland or how long he stayed, since there is a three-year period for which there is no record of him at all. He may have been invited to Holland as early as 1737 by Anna, Princess of Orange, to whom he dedicated his fourth book of sonatas. She was the patron of Pietro Locatelli, the Italian violinist and pupil of Corelli who was the leader of musical life in Holland; and it is assumed that she wished to bring about a meeting between him and Leclair. According to one account, which can not be satisfactorily substantiated, Leclair and Locatelli played together in the German city of Kassel in 1738. We do know that in 1740, Leclair was employed by François du Liz, a colorful adventurer, to play at his house in The Hague twice a week for five years at a large fee. But this contract was terminated in 1742, when du Liz became bankrupt.

No doubt Leclair and Locatelli, who had but few rivals in Europe, had much to say to each other, though which may have influenced the other more would be hard to say. The sonatas and concertos of Leclair, though technically advanced, do not make the extraordinary demands, some of which hardly could have been met even by their composer, of Locatelli's *L'Arte del violino*. On the other hand, Leclair's music has more distinctive melody and a more individual personality. It is recognizably French, though this is mainly attributable to a conscious use of rhythms such as that of the minuet and the *chasse*, a traditional French "hunting" piece. Still, there is a quality of elegance in Leclair's music that does reflect the great preoccupation of his time and place. In all, he composed, among other works, twelve concertos for three violins, viola, cello, and organ and forty-eight sonatas, of which the best known, probably, is the one he called *Le Tombeau*. This sonata is most familiar to us today in the arrangement by Ferdinand David, a notable violinist of the next century. The *Chaconne* of Leclair's Sonata, op. 5 no. 4, is an essay in the art of bowing. These works brought many technical innovations into French violin music, including multiple stops, an idiomatic use of the fourth position, downward breaking of chords, and the extended *crescendo* and *diminuendo*.

Leclair played in public but seldom after his early Paris years. Later on, when he held appointments to princes, he must have played at court functions. In 1743–44, he was at Chambéry after the conquest of that town from the Duke of Savoy by the combined French and Spanish forces. A court had been set up there by the Spanish Infante, Don Filippo, to whom Leclair dedicated his second book of concertos.

In 1744, Leclair returned to Paris for the composition and production of his one opera, *Scylla et Glaucus*, which was given on October 4, 1746, at the Académie Royale with a cast that included the star ballerina, Anna Camargo, and a popular soprano of the time, Mlle. Fell. The opera was dedicated to the Comtesse de la Mark, who was prominent in Paris society and was a talented amateur singer and *clavecinist*.

French opera had not gone very far since the days of Lully until 1737, despite the contributions of André Campra and the team of François Francoeur and François Rebel. However, in that year, the success of Jean Philippe Rameau's *Castor et Pollux* revitalized the form. It was probably the sudden triumph of Rameau, who had remained a provincial

organist until he was past fifty, that encouraged Leclair, who
was now almost that age, to turn to opera. But the experi-
ment was not successful enough to put him in a class with
Rameau; and in 1748, he accepted an appointment as first
violin to the Duc de Gramont at Puteaux, near Paris. He remained in this post, which was not a demanding one and
permitted him to live at home, for the rest of his life. His
duties included the arrangement of ballets and divertissements, some of which he composed himself, and he provided
music for all occasions, both formal and informal.

In 1758, Leclair, who appears to have become extremely
eccentric, left his wife and went to live in Courtille, a lowly
and sinister Paris suburb. His wife remained in comfortable
circumstances. The Duc de Gramont, alarmed at this turn of
events, asked Leclair to take up residence with him, but was
refused. Presumably, Leclair continued to serve his patron,
but otherwise remained a recluse. On the morning of October 22, 1764, he was found stabbed to death in his house.

No solution to this mysterious murder has ever been discovered, though the police made a thorough investigation at
the time. Several theories were put forward but none
proved.

When Leclair died—seven months after Locatelli died in
Holland—Diderot and d'Alembert were laboring on their
great *Encyclopédie,* Voltaire had just published his *Philo-
sophical Dictionary,* and people were secretly reading Rousseau's *Émile.* Two years earlier, Christoph Gluck had
produced his *Orfeo ed Eurydice* in Vienna, beginning his
revolution in opera. The *querre des buffons,* which, twelve
years before, had divided Paris between French *opera seria*
and Italian *opera buffa,* had led to the establishment of a
fashion that eventually produced the French *opéra-comique.*
André Grétry's *Le Tableau parlant,* produced three years
after Leclair's death, was the first work in a stream that
finally became a torrent.

Lully (originally an Italian), Rameau (who died a month
before Leclair), and Grétry (actually a Belgian) were the
creators of the French style in opera, while the creators of

the French style in instrumental music were François Couperin and Leclair. Couperin, who composed almost exclusively for the harpsichord and organ, did produce a famous work for the violin, his trio sonata *Le Parnasse, ou L'Apothéose de Corelli* (1724). Leclair, who settled in Paris five years before Couperin died in 1733, may or may not have known him; but he must have been conscious of him and his work when he tried to express in music the charm and elegance that, however superficial, were in his time, as they still are today, essentially French.

8

Johann Wenzel Stamitz

1717–1757

One of the great transitional figures in the history of music, Johann Wenzel Stamitz was strangely neglected until recent times, having been judged not for what he accomplished but in comparison to the accomplishments of those who came after him and for whom, in some respects, he paved the way.

Though he outlived his great predecessor, J. S. Bach, only by seven years, Stamitz was actually contemporary with Bach's sons, one of whom, Carl Philip Emmanuel Bach, shares with him the distinction of having developed the ultimate sonata form. C. P. E. Bach, together with Muzio Clementi, the Italian-English pianist and composer of the next generation, is credited with perfecting the keyboard sonata; but it was Stamitz who, more than any other, adapted the form for orchestral music and so gave to the symphony the structure and characteristics by which it has been known ever since.

The question of the national origins of the Stamitz family was the cause of much controversy, particularly at the time of Hitler's Third Reich, when the Stamitzes were claimed both by the Czechoslovak nationalists and the Sudeten Germans. The greatest authority on the Stamitz family and the Mannheim school, Dr. Peter Gradenwitz, was caught in the middle and much abused when he established that, though the name sometimes was given in Czech form as Stamic, it was not actually Czech or German. The fact that he proved beyond doubt that the family originally was Slovene, having come from Marburg, now the Yugoslav city of Maribor, was ignored, and Dr. Gradenwitz was accused of having played into the hands of Nazi propagandists. Now, however, the facts are clear and Dr. Gradenwitz's contributions to scholarship acknowledged and honored.

The first musical Stamitz, Anton, arrived in the town of Deutschbrod, now the Czechoslovak town of Havlíčkuv Brod, in 1710. He became established as an organist, conductor, and teacher, and married a wealthy landowner's daughter. Their first child, Jan Vaczlav Antonín, or Johann Wenzel Anton, was born on June 17 or 19, 1717. Ten more children were to follow. The next son, Joseph, became a well-known painter.

Whether Stamitz was trained as a violinist by his father or by one of the Jesuits with whom he studied is not known. He developed early and was a more than accomplished player at fourteen, when he was invited to play at the coronation of the Holy Roman Emperor, Charles VII, as King of Bohemia at Prague. This was a singular honor for so young a man and attracted much attention to him. There was no strong German school of violin playing at the time. The masters of the previous century, Johann Jakob Walther and Heinrich von Biber, had few successors in Germany. The Italian influence became strong, particularly through Vivaldi's pupil, Johann Georg Pisendel, a contemporary of Bach, who was, until his death in 1755, prominent at the court of the Elector of Saxony in Dresden. Among Stamitz's contemporaries, the only other German violinist of note was Franz Benda, who, like his teacher, J. G. Graun, was for many years violinist to Frederick the Great at Potsdam.

After Stamitz's appearance at the coronation in Prague, he was promptly hired for the orchestra of the Elector Palatine at Mannheim, where he was to make his name and, so far as music was concerned, make the name of Mannheim. So great was his talent and effect and so high his standing with the Elector, that by 1745, when he was only eighteen, he was leader of the orchestra and director of chamber music. The year before, he had married Maria Antonia Lüneborn. Their first son, Karl, was born in 1745, their daughter, Maria Francisca, in 1746, and their second son, Johann Anton, in 1754.

Mannheim, at the confluence of the Rhine and Neckar rivers, was a handsome planned city, built a century earlier on a gridiron pattern. The Elector's palace, an emulation of Versailles, was one of the largest baroque buildings in Europe. The Elector Palatine, thanks mainly to Stamitz, became an outstanding music patron of Europe. The opera house that he built, and inaugurated in 1742 to celebrate the marriage of his son, was one of the largest in Europe, seating five thousand people. It was destroyed by bombing in World War II.

The Mannheim style, which became famous in Stamitz's time and even more famous afterwards under his successor, Christian Cannabich, was largely Stamitz's creation. It had to do not only with the music played but with the way it was played. The orchestra consisted of twenty musicians, who, under Stamitz as first violin and leader, gradually changed from an old-fashioned ensemble that was used mainly for accompaniments to something resembling a modern orchestra. Stamitz emphasized accuracy of phrasing and uniformity of bowing. He also developed the effect of continuous *crescendo* that soon excited all of Europe. In his symphonies, of which he composed a total of seventy-four, fifty-five in his maturity, he made the significant step of eliminating the *continuo* or figured bass, played by the harpsichord. This was done by the use and development of middle voices in the orchestration. In adapting the still-developing sonata form to the symphony, he stressed the development section of the first movement, which now consisted of theme, development, and recapitulation. He also standardized the sequence of movements: *allegro, andante,* minuet, *presto.* The winds became more important in his orchestra, and the variety and scope of dynamics were greatly increased. Perhaps the most important characteristic of his symphonies, one that was to influence Haydn, Mozart, and eventually Beethoven, was the definite opposition of the themes in the opening movement, the first being strong and insistent and the contrasting subject songful, or *cantabile.* The characteristic opening theme became known as the "Mannheim rocket." A typical example is the opening theme of Beethoven's First Piano Sonata, op. 2 no. 1.

The music of the Mannheim school became known as the *melodia germanica,* for Stamitz abandoned counterpoint and in his symphonies acted as the bridge between Bach and Handel on the one hand and Haydn, Mozart, and Beethoven on the other.

In Stamitz's day, the conductor of the orchestra did not simply conduct but also played. In Stamitz's case, he conducted while playing the violin, though others of his time, such as C. P. E. Bach, conducted from the harpsichord. Busy as he was with his orchestra and composing symphonies for it, Stamitz also managed to compose seven violin sonatas, a number of trios, and several violin caprices, works that are unknown today but would be interesting to hear. One of his best-known works is the Concerto in B-flat for Clarinet, the first known concerto for that instrument. He also composed concertos for harpsichord, violin, flute, and oboe.

Stamitz left Mannheim only twice during his relatively short life. The first time, in 1749–50, he took a leave of absence to visit his large family in Bohemia. The second time, in 1754, he went to Paris, where he had been preceded by a great reputation. One of his symphonies had been played there at the *Concert spirituel* as early as 1751. The following year, he had become more famous in a curious way, for the strange contest between musical forces known as the *guerre des buffons,* in which the followers of Italian *opera buffa* were pitted against those of the traditional French *opera seria,* included a battle of witty pamphlets, the first of which,

Le petit prophète de Boehmischbroda, obviously had to do with Stamitz himself and his musical innovations. By the time he actually appeared at the *Concert spirituel,* on September 8, 1754, playing a sonata of his own not for violin but for *viola d'amore,* he was already something of a *cause celèbre.* One wonders if he chose to perform first on the *viola d'amore* because he had been warned that, despite the successes of Leclair and Guignon, the violin was not yet fully accepted as a solo instrument in Paris.

On March 22, 1755, one of Stamitz's symphonies was given at the *Concert spirituel,* and on August 4, his *Missa Solemnis,* employing all the forces of the *Concert spirituel,* was given its *première.* In the meantime, Stamitz had come under the patronage of M. Riche de la Pouplinière, who was the patron of the aging Rameau and at whose house he conducted concerts featuring his own symphonies. These private concerts must have given the musical and social elite of Paris its first taste of what was to come a few years later in the early works of Haydn and Mozart. One of the French composers on whom Stamitz had a direct influence was François Gossec, then only twenty, who began composing symphonies soon after Stamitz's Paris season.

Stamitz died a little more than a year after his return to Mannheim, on March 27, 1757. He was not yet forty. His son, Anton, entered the Mannheim orchestra in 1764 at the age of ten. His daughter, Maria Francisca, achieved some reputation as a singer and married Franz Lang, a member of the Mannheim orchestra. In later years, Anton settled in Paris and became a violin teacher. One of the pupils was to be Rodolphe Kreutzer. The older son, Karl, became a noted violinist, first with the Mannheim orchestra and later as a soloist in Germany, Paris, and Russia. He composed some seventy symphonies, modeled on those of his father but containing many advances developed from them. Ironically, some of these are better known today than any of his father's. Karl Stamitz also composed two operas and seven violin concertos, as well as many sonatas, quartets, and other chamber works. Thirteen years younger than Haydn and eleven years older than Mozart, he was overshadowed by both of them, as indeed, in the long run, was his father. But Haydn and Mozart each admitted their debt to Johann Wenzel Stamitz and to the Mannheim style that he created. Musicians who helped sustain the reputation of the Mannheim orchestra immediately after Stamitz's death were, besides Christian Cannabich, Anton Filtz, Franz Xavier Richter, and Ignaz Holzbauer, all of whom contributed to the development of the symphony.

9

Giovanni Battista Viotti

1755–1824

The English musicologist, Sir Donald Tovey, wrote in his essay on the composer Gluck: "The worst of musical history is that when the history is interesting the music is often disappointing without it, and when the music is great it often has no discernible history." So, the man who merely loves music can be enchanted by Haydn and bored by Stamitz without knowing, or, indeed, caring about Stamitz's historical development of the symphony. A case in point is that of Giovanni Battista Viotti, who has been called "the father of modern violin playing" and who developed the modern virtuoso violin concerto.

The great concertos of Haydn, Mozart, and Beethoven were composed during Viotti's lifetime, and while Viotti's concertos do not compare with them musically, one or two of them (particularly the twenty-second) are still performed occasionally. But Viotti set a model that was imitated slavishly in a stream of virtuoso concertos by the great violinists who came after him. Almost all of these concertos are now forgotten or are remembered only as curiosities; but in Viotti's day and for some years after, it was customary if not obliga-

tory for a virtuoso to perform his own works, whether he was
a pianist or violinist. The great virtuoso who was not also a
composer hardly existed until the end of the nineteenth century. And yet, the really enduring music for both piano and
violin—if one excepts Liszt and Paganini—was not composed by great performing virtuosos.

Viotti was born on May 23, 1755, at Fontonetto Po, near
Vercelli, in Italy's Piedmont. His father was a blacksmith
who played the horn. A roving lute player named Giovannini
gave him his first violin lessons. In 1763, Viotti's mother
died; and his father was married again soon afterwards.
Viotti developed a strong affection for his stepmother, which
endured for the rest of her life.

However, Viotti left home early, at the age of eleven, when
he was chosen by a nobleman, the Marchese di Vogliera, to
act as companion to his son, the Prince of Cisterna, at Turin.
Since the Prince was eighteen, he did not think much of having a boy seven years his junior for a companion. He was
about to send Viotti home when he accidentally discovered
his exceptional musical talents. Impressed, he arranged for
his father to become Viotti's patron and for him to study
with a violinist of the Piedmontese court, Antonio Celoniat,
who soon sent him to Gaetano Pugnani, a pupil of G. B.
Somis and himself an important teacher in the classic tradition of Corelli and Tartini. Inspired by Pugnani, a prolific
composer who became music director to the Piedmontese
court, Viotti made remarkable progress and had composed
his first solo concerto by the time he was fourteen. In 1770,
four years after he began training with Pugnani, he started
on his performing career. Accompanied by his teacher, he
went first to Geneva. He then made an extensive tour to
Dresden, Berlin (where he played for Frederick the Great),
Warsaw, and St. Petersburg. In Russia, where he remained
for some time, he attracted the interest of Prince Potemkin,
the favorite of Catherine the Great, for whom he performed.
Touring virtuosos were still a rarity in Russia, though after
the French Revolution, when Paris for a time ceased to be
the music capital of Europe, many performers found it

profitable to go there. St. Petersburg and, to a lesser extent, Moscow eventually rivaled London, Paris, and Vienna in attracting prominent performers.

Since the railroads did not come into general use until after Viotti's death, touring in his time meant long, slow journeys by ship or overland by coach. So an artist stayed as long as he profitably could in each city he visited.

Public concerts, often controlled by musical societies, were becoming established in various cities of Europe at this time. In London, the concerts given regularly by Johann Christian Bach and his partner, Karl Friedrich Abel, had begun their successful course in 1769, the year that Bach gave the first public performance on the pianoforte. In the same year, the *Concerts des amateurs* was added to the *Concert spirituel* in Paris. The *Grosses Konzert* had been in existence in Frankfort since 1740. The famous Leipzig concerts that later became known as the Gewandhaus concerts, after the building in which they were given, were founded by Johann Adam Hiller in 1763. The *Liebhaber Konzert* in Berlin began in the year before Viotti's arrival in that city. The concerts of the Tonkunstler Sozietät in Vienna date from 1771. In Amsterdam, the concerts of the Felix Meritis originated in 1777. All of these public concerts were bourgeois institutions and existed independently of those concerts sponsored by the ruling princes. Opera houses still were controlled by the princes in most cities, though in London, Hamburg, Venice, and some other cities, they were subsidized either by the city government or wealthy patrons.

In 1781, Viotti arrived in Paris, where he was to remain for a decade. He first appeared at the *Concert spirituel* on March 15, 1782, and for a time was leader of its orchestra. Viotti's fee as soloist was a hundred francs. Fifty years later, Paganini was to receive 15,000 francs for a similar appearance.

Though he immediately attracted attention and admiration, Viotti was not entirely successful in Paris, for he appears to have disliked performing in public and to have had a disdain for the public and for patrons. Like many another foreign performer, he failed to understand the French and their intrigues. In addition he was involved, involuntarily, in a rivalry with the violinist Isidore Berthaume, who also served as leader of the orchestra of the *Concert spirituel.*

Fortunately, though Viotti was dropped by the *Concert spirituel,* he immediately was taken up the by the Queen, Marie Antoinette, who granted him a pension. One of the stories published during Viotti's lifetime was that he decided to avoid public performances as much as possible after an episode at Versailles. While playing before the court, he was interrupted by the noisy entrance of the Comte d'Artois and his retinue. Daringly, Viotti stopped playing and, refusing to continue, left the room. Since he had the protection of the Queen, he got away with it. But he did not play in public again for several years, though his performances in private homes became famous and invitations to them were eagerly sought by the elite.

In 1785, Viotti took up residence with Luigi Cherubini, a young composer just arrived in Paris who was to become the most powerful man in the Parisian musical world and reign almost as dictator of all things musical until his death at the age of eighty-one in 1841. A fine composer but musical reactionary, he was a follower of Gluck and resisted all change, though he outlived Mozart, Weber, Beethoven, and Schubert and lived long enough to set himself against Liszt and Berlioz.

Viotti began a career as an impresario in 1788, when he was appointed manager jointly with the Queen's hairdresser, Léonard Autié, of the new Théâtre de Monsieur, which was patronized by the Comte de Provence, brother of King Louis XVI, and was located first in a salon of the Tuileries Palace. The same year, Viotti went to Italy to engage singers. The theater opened on January 26, 1789, with performances of Pergolesi's *La Serva padrona* and Giacomo Tritto's *Vicende amorose.* Leader of the orchestra was Viotti's contemporary, Niccolo Mestrino, a popular violinist in Paris who had served the Esterházy princes in Hungary under Haydn and who supposedly had perfected his violin technique while serving a prison term.

After the fall of the Bastille on July 14, 1789, Viotti's theater was moved to another location and its name changed to Théâtre Feydeau. On February 1, 1790, Viotti reappeared at a public performance, playing the *première* of his Fourteenth Concerto in his own theater. His partner, Léonard Autié, fled France at this time; but Viotti continued as manager. In 1791, he gave the *première* of Cherubini's opera, *Lodoïska,* in competition with another opera on the same subject, given at the same time in another theater, by Rodolphe Kreutzer. The Théâtre Feydeau, which, despite Viotti's best efforts, had never been successful, was closed down later the same year.

Though many fled earlier, Viotti, who, whatever his political sentiments, was sincerely devoted to Marie Antoinette (a frivolous queen, perhaps, but well trained musically), remained in Paris until after the arrest of the King and Queen. We do not know exactly when he left Paris or whether he took refuge somewhere else before arriving in England at the end of 1792.

At the time of the French Revolution, which shook Europe to its depths and destroyed the absolute power if not the institution of feudal aristocracy, as well as the belief in the divine right of kings, musicians throughout Europe still were largely dependent on patrons. Because fashion was controlled by the privileged few and imitated by the *nouveau riche,* tastes were slow to change, at least in music. Though Christoph Gluck found success in Paris as early as 1774, when his *Iphigénie en Aulide* was produced at the Opéra, the effects of his operatic reform were not fully to be felt until after the Revolution. The music of Haydn and Mozart had little influence outside of Vienna until the last decade of the eighteenth century.

Haydn, who had a secure and reasonably easy life, thanks to the patronage of the Esterházy princes, was probably the only composer of consequence before the nineteenth century who was not also a performing virtuoso. Mozart, whose father was a fine violinist and author of one of the earliest violin methods, was primarily a keyboard player and finally adopted the newly established pianoforte in preference to the clavichord or harpsichord in about 1780. His concertos for pianoforte, most of which were composed for his own use, are among his most glorious works; but they are not, strictly speaking, despite their many difficulties, virtuoso concertos. Nor are the five lovely violin concertos that he composed in the year 1775, when he was nineteen. These works represent the classical solo concerto at its apogee, in which solo passages are equal and contain new musical ideas rather than merely embellishing those presented in the orchestral *tuttis*. Mozart, who was himself an excellent violinist and disappointed his father by preferring the pianoforte, composed his violin concertos for his own use and that of Gaetano Brunetti, concertmaster of the Salzburg court orchestra. Some seven years before, the composer Luigi Boccherini had provided a concerto for the violinist Filippino Manfredi, with whom he toured in Italy, France, and Spain. This concerto apparently influenced Mozart, just as the clavier concertos of Carl Philipp Emmanuel Bach and his brother, Johann Christian Bach, had influenced him earlier and the Mannheim style in orchestral playing was to influence him two years later.

The French school of violin playing came into its own at the end of the eighteenth century as a direct result of Viotti's influence on his pupils, particularly Pierre Rode. Certain previous developments were important in its growth since the time of Leclair. In 1761, an important treatise by one of Leclair's pupils was published. This was *Principes du violon* by L'Abbé *le fils,* whose real name was Joseph Bernabé Saint-Sevin. His treatise had more in common with the one by Geminiani, published in England in 1751, than that of Leopold Mozart, which appeared five years later. L'Abbé *le fils* advocated holding the violin in a position similar to the one that now prevails, and detailed the use of harmonics. Leopold Mozart was aware of harmonics but warned against them.

Geminiani did not refer to them. Though natural harmonics had been used to a limited extent before 1750, it was not until then that their possibilities were really explored, chiefly as a result of *Les Sons Harmonique,* op. 4, by Jean Joseph de Mondonville, a violinist and composer who played in the orchestra of the *Concert spirituel* and at the time of his death in 1772, was choirmaster of the royal chapel at Versailles.

Instruction manuals for the violin began to appear frequently during the time of Leclair, when amateurs were beginning to take up the violin and its sister instruments in preference to the viols. The violin was at last becoming respectable, having proved itself over two centuries. Probably the most important of the instruction manuals were those by Michel Corette, particularly his *L'École de Orphée,* published in 1738. The famous flute treatise, published in 1752, by Johann Joachim Quantz, court composer to Frederick the Great, who was a flutist himself, contains valuable comments on violin bowings, particularly for orchestral players.

Others who preceded Viotti in Paris and were contemporary with or somewhat younger than Leclair were Louis Guillemain, whose music calls for bowing techniques in advance of Leclair's, and the violinist known only as Tremais, an advanced technician who worked up to the twelfth position and specialized in *scordatura* and multiple stops. Perhaps the most successful French violinist of the generation between Leclair and Viotti was Pierre Gavinès of Bordeaux, who was largely self-taught. Appearing at the *Concert spirituel* as early as 1741, he later directed the concerts. For the five years previous to his death in 1800, he taught at the newly founded Paris Conservatoire, the great institution that was created in 1795 and was one of the demonstrably good results of the French Revolution. Another violinist of this interim period was the Chevalier de Saint Georges, a mulatto from Guadeloupe. A pupil of Leclair, he had a reputation for eccentricity and, while a sound performer and composer, probably anticipated Paganini by appealing to the public as a curiosity or exotic.

Though romanticism did not manifest itself in music

until the nineteenth century, it had its literary beginnings much earlier. It was probably a novel by the German philosopher, Johann Wolfgang von Goethe, *The Sorrows of Werther,* published in 1774 and avidly read throughout Europe, that sparked the movement that was to unseat classicism. It is interesting to note that one of the first musical treatments of the Goethe novel was that of Gaetano Pugnani, Viotti's teacher. He called it *Werther, a Novel Set to Music,* and it was produced at Turin in 1796, two years before his death.

The extraordinary reputation of the Stradivari violins, particularly those of the last great master of that family, Antonio Stradivari, who died in 1737, was established by Viotti, who introduced them to Paris about 1775. He owned a particularly fine Stradivarius of 1712 and another of 1704 that later was known as the "Betts," a name it acquired from a dealer who bought it. Viotti apparently encouraged his colleagues and pupils to get possession of instruments by the Cremona masters, thus giving impetus to the boom that has continued, with ever-rising prices, until the present day.

Viotti made his London debut, performing the *première* of his Twenty-first Concerto, on February 7, 1793. The same year, he returned briefly to Italy to settle affairs after the death of his stepmother. In 1794 and 1795, he played in the series of concerts given by the orchestra under Johann Peter Salomon at which symphonies and other works by Haydn and Mozart were introduced to London. Haydn himself made his second visit to London during this time and conducted symphonies that he composed specially for these concerts. He was then sixty-three and at the height of his powers.

During the same year, Viotti also was leader of the orchestra of the Italian Opera at the King's Theatre and played in the first London performance of Gluck's *Alceste.* On May 29, 1794, a performance was given of Giovanni Paisiello's *La Serva padrona* into which was interpolated a song by Viotti, *La Polacca,* that became enormously popular.

In 1798, after playing frequently in public concerts, Viotti

again became leader at the King's Theatre, succeeding a
popular violinist, Wilhelm Cramer. Trained in the Mannheim
Orchestra and a pupil of Johann Wenzel Stamitz, Cramer
settled in London in 1772 and eventually was appointed
leader of the King's Band. His son, Johann Baptist Cramer,
born in 1771, became one of the great pianists of his time
and was known as "Glorious John."

From the time of Geminiani to that of Viotti, few violinists
had captured London audiences. Probably the most successful was a pupil of G. B. Somis, Felice de' Giardini, who died
at the age of eighty in 1796 and was still active as a player
and impresario of a comic-opera troupe in London as late as
1791. Other immediate predecessors of Viotti's who were
prominent in London concert life were the French-Irish violinist, François-Hippolyte Barthélemon, who married the
popular singer, Mary Young, with whom he gave concerts in
London, and Matthew Duborg, a pupil of Geminiani, who
died in 1769.

Soon after assuming his post at the King's Theatre in
1798, Viotti was accused of revolutionary activities and
given twenty-four hours to leave England. He was at this
time living in the house of friends, Mr. and Mrs. Chinnery,
and they suggested that he go to a friend of theirs in Germany. So he spent the next three years in Schönfeld near
Hamburg. During this period, he remained in obscurity,
though it is known that he gave lessons to a player in his
early teens, Friedrich Wilhelm Pixis, who became a noted
violinist and the first professor of violin at the Prague Conservatory, which was founded in 1811.

In 1801, Viotti was permitted to return to London, probably as the result of efforts on the part of the Chinnerys. At
this time, he began his ill-fated venture as a wine merchant,
financed by the devoted Chinnerys. Such ventures were not
then unusual for musicians, for public concerts were not
that frequently given or wealthy patrons and pupils that easy
to come by. Even so important a post as leader of the Italian
Opera did not in itself provide an adequate living.

Viotti did, for a few years at least, continue to play in public. On November 25, 1803, he played the *première* of his Twenty-third Concerto in London. For the next fifteen years, he traveled between London and Paris, sometimes performing, though always less frequently, teaching, composing, and working at the business of a wine merchant. In 1813, he played under the leadership of J. P. Salomon and the now-celebrated pianist, Muzio Clementi, at the first concerts of the newly formed Philharmonic Society of London, the oldest symphonic organization in the world, which still exists as the Royal Philharmonic. In 1814, he replaced the famous soprano, Angelica Catalani, as director of the Théâtre Italien in Paris. Again, he was unsuccessful as an impresario and soon gave up the post, or was replaced.

In 1818, the wine business to which Viotti had given so much time and attention, and on which he had pinned such hopes, failed, and he was ruined financially. Having lived throughout the Napoleonic era, he returned to the Paris of the Restoration and was appointed director of the Italian Opera of Louis XVIII, who was his former patron, the Comte de Provence. But the assassination of the King's nephew, the Duc de Berry, in the opera house on February 13, 1820, resulted in the closing of it and all the other theaters in France. Bad luck continued to pursue Viotti. He became manager of two other theaters in Paris, after they reopened, but was unable to produce anything but failures. Finally, in 1822, he received a small pension from the Opéra and returned to London. He died there in the house of Mrs. Chinnery, now a widow, on March 3, 1824. His greatest anxiety at the end came from the fact that he owed Mrs. Chinnery 24,000 francs, a sum that five or six years later Paganini could earn with one or two concerts.

Viotti's concertos, which followed strict sonata form and used more developed orchestral accompaniments, reflect the austere classical tone of the Revolutionary period. They anticipate the "dialogues" or sometimes "contests" between the soloist and the orchestra that became characteristic of the virtuoso concerto. All but a few of the many works in this genre that were composed by Viotti and his followers have faded with time and now are known, if at all, only to students. But for almost a century, they were the warhorses of the violinist's repertory. None of Viotti's other compositions, which, besides the twenty-nine violin concertos, include ten piano concertos, seven sets of string quartets, twelve violin sonatas and nine piano sonatas, six trios for two violins and bass, and four books of duets for violin, are known to us today, though a few have been recorded. One of his most celebrated performances at private concerts was that of his arrangement of the *Ranz des vaches,* a haunting Alpine melody that Berlioz later used in his *Symphonie fantastique.*

Strange to say, the great violinist-composers of the baroque era—Corelli, Vivaldi, Tartini, Veracini—have been revived, chiefly through recordings; but a similar revival of the later composers of virtuoso concertos has not taken place. Perhaps the music of Viotti, Rode, Kreutzer, Lipinski, Spohr, and their counterparts who composed for the piano, such as Moscheles, Hummel, Thalberg, and Herz, is lacking in quality to compare with that of their predecessors. The virtuoso element is no longer enough, as it was in the days when, still a novelty, it was an attraction in itself.

It was Viotti who introduced and may have had some influence upon the violin bow of François Tourte, who perfected it about 1775. Another bow maker, the Englishman John Dodd, may have developed a similar bow independently at about the same time. But Tourte (whose father was also a bow maker) is given credit for and gave his name to the bow that has become standard, fixing the basic design and setting the length (for violins) at twenty-nine and a half inches. He also discovered that the best wood is Pernambuco, corrected the balance of the bow head, raised the center of balance farther toward the point, and widened the ribbon of hair. Tourte never signed his bows, though John Dodd did.

Viotti probably was, as so many historians say, the greatest violinist before Paganini. Since that master did not perform outside Italy until 1828, Viotti never heard him, though very likely he heard of him. As the last exponent of the clas-

Seventeenth century Dutch harlequins playing the viola da gamba and the violin.

Jean-Baptiste Lully.

Francesco Maria Veracini.

Giuseppe Tartini.

Niccoló Paganini, with his autograph, showing his characteristic stance while playing (sketch by Sir Edwin Landseer).

Ole Bull instructing a pupil.

Joseph Joachim and Clara Schumann performing at a concert in Berlin in 1854 (after the watercolor by Adolph Menzel).

"Farewell" (Sarasate) J: Dinsdale del:

Pablo de Sarasate at a farewell performance.

sical school, which he inherited from Corelli through Somis
and Pugnani, he probably would have preferred the playing
of his pupil, Rode, or his disciple, Baillot—the two great
founders of the French school—to that of Paganini. Viotti
was of a school and influenced a school, while Paganini was
a law unto himself, a phenomenon that appeared to come
out of nowhere and disappeared from whence it came.

10

Rodolphe Kreutzer

1766–1831

To the average music lover, Kreutzer is only a name, familiar through the marvelous violin sonata that Beethoven dedicated to Rodolphe Kreutzer. His name was also immortalized in literature in 1889, when the Russian novelist, Leo Tolstoy, published a short novel entitled *The Kreutzer Sonata*. To violin students, however, Kreutzer's forty études (or caprices) for the violin are what the études of Carl Czerny are to the piano student.

The eighteenth century was the century of the violin, while the nineteenth was to be the century of the piano. In his études, Kreutzer summarized the entire range of violin technique, which had been evolving for almost three centuries, while Czerny, who was twenty-five years younger than Kreutzer, did the same for piano technique, which evolved much more quickly. Kreutzer, it might be said, prepared the ground for a Paganini, while Czerny prepared the ground for a Liszt.

Naturally, Kreutzer did not stand alone, but was one of several violinists who made the French school the model for virtuoso violin technique. The most important immediate influence was that of G. B. Viotti. Though Kreutzer never actually studied with him, he was profoundly affected by hearing Viotti play in Paris before the French Revolution.

Born in Versailles on November 16, 1766, Kreutzer was the son of a violinist of the royal chapel. He studied first with his father, who died when Kreutzer was sixteen, and then with Anton Stamitz, the son of Johann Wenzel Stamitz, the leader of the Mannheim school. After the death of his father, Kreutzer was appointed to the royal chapel in his place through the influence of the Queen, Marie Antoinette. It was at this time that he attended concerts given by Viotti. Though he did receive instruction, Kreutzer had the reputation of being naturally gifted to such an extent that he learned more by example than anything else.

In 1790, Kreutzer became solo violinist at the Théâtre Italien in Paris, thus beginning his long association with opera, which was to be his chief preoccupation. Stage works became tremendously important during the Revolution and the years that followed it. Classicism was the style that expressed the times, since the noble ideals of Greek democracy and its Roman counterpart inspired and supported those of the Revolution. Kreutzer's first opera, produced on May 10, 1790, ten months after the fall of the Bastille, was *Jeanne d'Arc à Orléans*, a subject both popular and safe. That work was followed, on January 15, 1791, by *Paul et Virginie*, which was to prove the most popular of Kreutzer's more than forty operas. On August 1, 1791, he produced his *Lodoïska* in competition with another opera on the same subject by Luigi Cherubini, produced at the same time by Viotti at the Théâtre Feydeau. During the revolutionary years, Kreutzer produced several operas on popular subjects that had, at least indirectly, the proper connotations. Two of these were *Werther et Charlotte*, after Goethe, and *Cymbeline*, after Boccaccio. During the reign of terror, he was one of twelve composers who together concocted an antiroyalist opera called *Le Congrès des rois*, which, though it took the line proper at the moment, lasted but one performance. Some of the other composers involved were Cherubini, Grètry, who had been forced to turn his comic talents to making fun of religion, Nicolas Delayrac, a pioneer of *opéra-comique*, and Étienne-Nicolas Méhul, then just beginning his career. Méhul was to become composer extraordinary to the Revolution.

When the Paris Conservatoire was formed from two existing schools in 1795, Kreutzer was appointed a professor of violin, together with Pierre Gavinès, who died in 1800. At first, the direction of the Conservatoire was shared by the composer François Gossec, Bernard Sarrette, whose school for army musicians gave impetus to the founding of the Conservatoire, Grétry, Méhul, and Cherubini. Sarrette was the strongest force during the early years; but after the Napoleonic era, the indestructible Cherubini was director and virtual dictator for some twenty years.

Also appointed as a violin professor at the Conservatoire was another notable violinist of the period, Pierre Jacques Joseph Rode. Born in Bordeaux on February 15, 1774, he was seven years younger than Kretuzer but died a year earlier. After six years' training in Bordeaux with the violinist Fauvel, Rode became a pupil of Viotti in Paris, where he made his debut in 1790, the year in which he became leader of the second violins at Viotti's Théâtre Feydeau. At the time of his appointment to the Conservatoire in 1795, he was solo violinist at the Opéra. In later years, he was solo violinist to Napoleon (when he was first consul) and toured extensively in Europe, spending considerable time in both Spain and Russia. His powers declined drastically after 1808. He composed twenty-four violin *études* that are still in use and some thirteen violin concertos that are not. His best-known composition was his Variations in G, which became a vocal showpiece for singers of the time such as the illustrious Angelica Catalani, who is reputed to have been the highest-paid singer in history.

In 1796, Kreutzer began an extensive and very successful concert tour that took him to Italy (where he was much impressed by the playing of a fourteen year old prodigy, Niccolò Paganini), Germany, the Netherlands, and finally to Vienna, where he met Beethoven. However, the *Kreutzer* Sonata was not composed until four or five years later. Beethoven himself first performed the sonata in public in Vienna on May 24, 1802, together with the violinist George Polgreen Bridgetower. They gave at least one further public performance of it.

According to some historians, Beethoven intended to dedicate his sonata to Bridgetower but, having quarreled with him, gave the accolade to Kreutzer. Bridgetower, who, before coming to Vienna, had been leader of the Prince Regent's Pavillion Orchestra at Brighton in England, was a mulatto, born in 1779 in Poland of an African father and European mother. In some sources, his name is given not as Bridgetower but Bridgewater. A brilliant player, he apparently inspired Beethoven to create the *Kreutzer* Sonata, which many players of the time, including even Kreutzer himself, pronounced unplayable. Indeed, Kreutzer, who must have been a stern classicist in the mold of Viotti and Cherubini, hardly approved of Beethoven's music and reputedly fled the hall with his hands over his ears at first hearing the master's Second Symphony. This was some years after his visit to Vienna and his meeting with Beethoven. His reaction was not unique; in fact, it was commonplace. Even François Habaneck, the violinist-conductor who from 1826 pioneered for Beethoven's music in Paris, "corrected" the harmony in his symphonies, rearranged the movement sequences, and sometimes even took a movement from one symphony and inserted it into another. It was only after a vigorous propaganda campaign conducted by two advanced composers of the next generation, Liszt and Berlioz, that Beethoven's music was played in Paris as he intended it to be.

Kreutzer once said, in answer to an appeal to play something by Berlioz at one of the concerts at the Opéra that he supervised: "What would happen to us if we helped newcomers?" This remark does not seem so surprising when it is realized that Kreutzer was used to playing it safe and had learned how in a hard school, having somehow managed to survive and hold his position in the musical world of Paris through all the twists and turns of the *ancien régime,* the Revolution, the Directory, the Empire, and, finally, the Restoration. Though only four years Beethoven's senior, he belonged with the followers of Gluck, headed by Cherubini, who were once revolutionaries in music, but, after a quarter-century of change and development, had become reactionaries. Kreutzer, though in a sense a rival of Cherubini's in the struggle for public esteem, actually belonged with him and composed in a vein similar to his. Unfortunately, particularly in Paris, members of the musical establishment felt compelled to hold the line against all invaders, defending the past by resisting the future. But we who are gifted with the hindsight of history should not criticize too much, for had we lived then, we might very well have covered our ears to escape Beethoven's harmonies or hissed and booed one of Berlioz's overtures.

At the time of their meeting in 1798, Kreutzer was—in the eyes of the world, at least—a more important personage than Beethoven. Certainly, he enjoyed in his lifetime more power and prestige than Beethoven. Though often in financial difficulties, Beethoven became increasingly revered in Vienna and, at the end of his life, had some fame in other countries, though his music was apt to be more talked about than played. Although the great Ninth Symphony was commissioned by the Philharmonic Society of London, his music, which became more and more introspective, was slow to gain acceptance; and his status as one of the supreme musical thinkers of the Western World was not recognized until long after his death in 1827.

One of the leading musicians of Vienna in the early 1800's was the violinist Franz Clement, who was ten years younger than Beethoven and lived until 1842. He served as violinist to the imperial court and from 1802 to 1811 was leader of the orchestra at the Theater an der Wien, where he gave regular subscription concerts and led opera and *Singspiel* performances. This theater was the setting for the *première* of Beethoven's only opera, *Fidelio,* on November 20, 1805, with the composer conducting from the piano. It has been

planned to serve again as the setting for a *Fidelio* production
in 1970 to celebrate the two hundredth anniversary of the
composer's birth, with American Leonard Bernstein scheduled to conduct.

Beethoven's *Eroica* Symphony was first performed at one
of Clement's subscription concerts in the Theater an der
Wien on April 7, 1805. At a later concert, on December 23,
1806, Clement was the soloist in the first performance of the
Beethoven Violin Concerto in D, composed for him but dedicated to the composer's lifelong friend, Stephan von Breun-
ing. Clement played the work at sight without a rehearsal
and after the first movement, provided an interlude in which
he performed his own Sonata on One String with the Violin
Reversed. Such interpolations were common practice in
those days. The Concerto in D, one of the towering master-
pieces of the violin literature, was hardly ever performed
again until it was revived in 1833 by the Belgian master,
Henri Vieuxtemps, and then in 1844 by the Hungarian prodigy, Joseph Joachim, who finally made it popular.

Again at the Theater an der Wien, on December 22, 1808,
Beethoven participated in another of Clement's concerts at
which he conducted the *premières* of his Fifth and Sixth
Symphonies and played the first performance of his Fourth
Piano Concerto. As for Clement, he became conductor of the
Vienna Hofoper from 1818 to 1821 and in later years, toured
extensively in concert, sometimes with the celebrated so-
prano, Catalani.

It seems apparent that, in composing his Violin Concerto,
Beethoven was using as his examples the virtuoso concertos
of Viotti, Kreutzer, and Rode, which aspired to a lofty and
noble classicism but, unlike Beethoven's concerto, are all
manner with very little content. Beethoven had studied both
the violin and the viola and, unlike many composers who
were primarily pianists, needed no professional advice on
how to compose for string instruments. In 1794, soon after
his arrival in Vienna from Bonn, he had lessons from the
violinist Ignaz Shuppanzigh, who was then leader of the
quartet maintained by Prince Carl Lichnowsky. From 1808

to 1816, he was leader of the quartet maintained by Count (later Prince) Andreas Rasumovsky, the Russian ambassador in Vienna, to whom Beethoven dedicated the three wonderful quartets of his Opus 59. Shuppanzigh, whom Beethoven called Falstaff because he was so fat, led the quartet in first performances of many of Beethoven's chamber works. After 1823, he also was associated with Franz Schubert in first performances of some of his chamber works.

Beethoven also had associations with Kreutzer's colleague, Pierre Rode, who appeared in Vienna in 1816. His reputation had preceded him; and Beethoven hastened to complete his tenth and last Violin Sonata, op. 96, so that Rode could play it. The first performance took place at the house of Prince Franz Joseph von Lobkowitz, one of the three aristocratic patrons who granted Beethoven a subsidy (the others were Prince Kinsky and the Archduke Rudolph). Rode played the sonata with the Archduke Rudolph, who was an excellent amateur. Unfortunately, Rode was by this time well past his prime as a player; and the performance was disappointing to Beethoven, who had composed the last movement of the sonata in a manner to please Rode. He later suggested to the Archduke Rudolph that before he and Rode played the sonata again, he should tactfully submit the score to Rode for further study.

The Archduke Rudolph, who was the half-brother of the Austrian Emperor, Franz I, received many dedications from Beethoven, including the sonata that he played with Rode and the Fifth or *Emperor* Piano Concerto. Since the Archduke never became the Emperor but instead finished his life as Cardinal-Archbishop of Olmütz, it is not clear why the Fifth Piano Concerto acquired that title, unless it somehow evolved as a means of describing the majesty of the music. The *Missa Solemnis*, one of the great last works of Beethoven, was intended for performance at the ceremonies attendant upon the Archduke's installation as Archbishop, but was not completed until four years after that event.

Prince Lobkowitz, to whom Beethoven dedicated his first

quartets, Opus 18, the *Eroica* Symphony, the Triple Concerto, and the song cycle, *An die ferne Geliebte,* was an amateur singer, violinist, and cellist, and for a while was director of the Hofoper. Prince Carl Lichnowsky, one of Beethoven's early patrons, presented to him the Guarnerius violin and cello, the Amati violin, and a viola dating from 1690 that are now in the Beethovenhaus at Bonn.

By this time, a fashionable craze for the piano was taking hold in Vienna. Talented amateurs, both male and female, of the aristocracy and the wealthy bourgeoisie abounded, as everywhere else in Europe; and so there was an even greater demand for chamber music than in Mozart's day. The role of the piano in sonatas, trios, quartets, and quintets was freely developed by Beethoven, who, of course, also developed the string quartet far beyond the lines laid down by Haydn and Mozart.

In Paris, Kreutzer succeeded Rode as solo violinist at the Opéra, and from 1817 to 1824 conducted the Opéra and directed its concerts. His career as a violinist had ended in 1810, when he broke an arm. He continued as violin professor at the Conservatoire until 1825 and in 1826 retired from all of his activities. He died in Geneva on June 6, 1831. In addition to his many operas and the violin études, he left nineteen violin concertos, three double concertos, and a number of chamber works. His successor at the Conservatoire, beginning in 1826, was his brother and pupil, Jean Nicolas Auguste Kreutzer, also a fine violinist. Auguste's son, Léon Kreutzer, became a noted critic and music historian as well as an able composer.

After 1802, Kreutzer and Rode had as their associate at the Conservatoire another celebrated violinist of the period, Pierre Marie François de Sales Baillot. Together, the three men prepared the *méthode de violon,* published in 1803, which became the official violin method of the Conservatoire and was an important influence on many of the virtuosos who came after them.

Baillot, who was born in 1771 and died in 1842, was five years younger than Kreutzer. Though never a pupil of Viotti, he was one of his disciples, having heard him play first at the age of ten. Soon afterwards, when his father died, he was sent to Rome as companion to the children of a government official and there studied with Pollani, a pupil of Pietro Nardini. Returning to Paris, he made his debut there in 1795 in a concerto by Viotti. He subsequently was a member of Napoleon's private band, toured extensively to much acclaim, and spent some time at the Russian court. Known as the last great violinist of the classical school and an estimable ensemble player, he became very active in organizing chamber-music concerts and promoting the chamber literature. He composed nine concertos and many other works. His influence at the Paris Conservatoire was even greater than that of Kreutzer and Rode, since he survived them both by more than ten years. His son, René Paul de Sales Baillot, who lived until 1889, was for many years professor of ensemble at the Conservatoire.

Though it could be said that the classical school of violin playing ended abruptly in 1828, when Paganini came out of Italy to conquer Europe, the evolution of violin technique actually owes less to him and more to Viotti and his followers. The violinists of the future, though they may have tried hard to imitate Paganini, knew what they did and did what they could chiefly because of the example and teaching of Kreutzer, Rode, and Baillot.

II

Nicolò Paganini

1782–1840

The Paganini legend, created with the help of the great violinist himself, grew to fantastic proportions. However, common sense and modern scholarship have put it in proper perspective at last; and we can now separate the real man from the grotesquely distorted myth.

Perhaps it is true that interest in Paganini has faded in this modern age, now that we know better than to believe that his gifts were supernaturally derived. Any of a dozen contemporary violinists could reproduce his technical feats, though probably only one or two could approach him in other ways. Even so, there has been only one Paganini, for in him the man and his times together produced a phenomenon. His impact, obviously extraordinary, was in many ways extra-musical, though he undoubtedly was—contrary opinions notwithstanding—a true musician. He had that rarest of qualities, which is hard to define but is a combination of talent, technique, and personality, that can best be described in modern jargon as the ability to "turn on" his listeners. And he lived at a time when people, for rea-

sons that were social, political, economical, and psychologi-
cal, were ready, willing, and able to be "turned on."

Revolution and the Napoleonic conquests unsettled and
aroused the whole of Europe, bringing changes, both superficial and profound. Hero worship was very strong then. A
new romanticism was in the air. Old habits of thought no
longer sustained those who had them and had no appeal to
those whose habits were unformed. Pleasures once available
only to those born to them were now available to anybody
who could pay for them. Idealism that inspired only a few
still affected the many. Religion, taken for granted, had
relaxed its hold on the minute details of life. Somber and
terrible events, which, after all, were always taking place
and always had, were met by a new frivolity that the old
ruling classes had bestowed upon the new.

Such was the mood of the times that created the Paganini
legend. Though he himself suffered as a result of his legend,
he knew the value of it, worked at living up to it, often
laughed and sometimes cursed at it, made attempts to act
against it, and believed implicitly in certain parts of it.

The legend began, as Paganini himself stated, in this
way: "The Savior appeared to my mother in a dream and
told her that a prayer should be fulfilled to her; she requested
that her son should become a great violinist and this was
granted her." If this was a romantic fabrication, it was not
Paganini's but his mother's, for he believed it and so, apparently, did she, and from a time long before his first successes.

Paganini was born in Genoa, in a small apartment in a
house near the waterfront, on October 27, 1782. Mozart then
had less than nine years to live and Beethoven was twelve
years old. The French Revolution was seven years off. Paganini's father, Antonio, had some musical ability and played
the mandolin after a fashion. His mother, who was born
Teresa Bocciardo, was religious, loving, and blindly loyal to
her family. Paganini, conforming to the admirable Italian
trait of honoring one's parents, would never speak ill of his
father and was purposely vague about him. When asked by a

biographer about his father's profession, he said that he was "a business man who was not wealthy." Actually, Antonio Paganini appears to have been an unstable character who was always waiting to win the lottery and was otherwise on the lookout for riches he did not have to earn.

When Paganini was four, he suffered the first of his many debilitating illnesses and was given up for dead. His mother considered that his sudden return to consciousness, just as burial arrangements were being made, was a miracle. Throughout his life, he had to overcome devastating attacks of pain and nausea and sometimes was laid low for months. He often played before huge audiences in so weakened a condition that he collapsed at the end of the concert.

Antonio Paganini seized upon his son's gifts, obvious when quite young, as his great hope in life. He was a stern, even cruel taskmaster, though Paganini would never say so. One of his disciplines was to starve the child if he had not been sufficiently diligent or had given displeasure in some other way. But he was shrewd enough to realize that his talented son needed good training and so somehow persuaded a theater violinist, Giovanni Servetto, to give him lessons, probably for free. Soon, the young Paganini came under the tutelage of Giacomo Costa, *maestro di cappella* of the Cathedral of San Lorenzo, and attracted the attention of a local opera composer, Francesco Gnecco, who introduced him as a precocious player to the musical society of Genoa. He played in churches while still only eight or nine, and soon his reputation began to spread throughout the city. His formal debut took place in Genoa when he was eleven at a concert given by two of the leading singers of the day, Teresa Bertinotti and Luigi Marchesi.

Paganini's first concert contributed to the legend, for it contained some of the elements that were to become standard. The boy was a sensation, not only because he was so young (he was advertised as being nine) and already played so brilliantly, but because of the piece that he performed—a set of variations on a Provençal folksong, *Carmagnole,* a song familiar at that time in a version with revolutionary overtones to the words. Whether it was his father or one of his sponsors who hit upon the piece we do not know. But this being the year 1793, when the French Revolution was in full swing, the choice was a shrewd move, considering the cheers it and the young Paganini evoked.

After this first concert, Paganini received the patronage of the Marchese di Negro, who thought that he should seek more advanced training somewhere outside Genoa. It was three years before the Marchese's advice was acted upon, for Paganini's father, for reasons we can not deduce, procrastinated. In 1795, another concert was given, this time with the young prodigy as star, to raise money for his musical education. In 1796, the noted violinist and composer, Rodolphe Kreutzer, came to Genoa. Paganini played for him, and Kreutzer was properly impressed, though it is unlikely that he suspected that, long after his own performing career had come to an end, young Paganini would become the rage of Europe.

Finally, in 1796, Antonio Paganini took his son to Parma, stopping first at Florence for a fund-raising concert. The trip to Parma was to seek lessons from Alessandro Rolla, leader of the court band and a celebrated violinist and teacher. Arriving unannounced at Rolla's house, the Paganinis were told that he was ill and could not see them. The young Paganini spied the manuscript of a new concerto by Rolla lying on a table and proceeded to play it at sight, thus flabbergasting its composer on his sickbed. Paganini later denied that he ever was taught by Rolla, who evidently thought that there was nothing he could teach him and advised lessons in counterpoint and composition instead. These he received from a court musician named Ghiretti and later from Ferdinand Paër, who was in Parma composing an opera for the Duke. Paër insisted on giving Paganini lessons twice a day for as long as he was in Parma. Years later, Paër was to become the teacher in Paris of another prodigy, Franz Liszt.

After some months in Parma, during which he played several times at court, Paganini, accompanied by his father, went on a concert tour of Milan, Bologna, Florence, Pisa,

Leghorn, and a few smaller cities. Returning to Genoa in 1797 with a sum of money sufficient to maintain the family for a while, he spent almost a year in seclusion, practicing rigorously and experimenting with double harmonics, bowing, and such special effects as multiple stops, left-hand *pizzicato,* and rapid *staccato* passages, for which he later was to become famous. During this period, he suffered again from illness, which probably was brought on by overwork and the nervous tension that resulted from conflict with his father.

We do not know how or why Paganini made the break with his father, but at the end of 1797 he left Genoa to play at the festival of St. Martin in Lucca. Though at first accompanied by his older brother, Luigi, he soon was, at the age of fifteen, completely on his own. Obviously, this is what he wanted and what he achieved, though not without the consciousness of being the only reliable support of his family.

Freedom went to the young man's head, and for a while he lived a dissolute life. He became a reckless gambler and something of a Don Juan, thus storing up tales for his future legend. Though he ceased to gamble after a few years, he was to bear the reputation of a gambler for the rest of his life. Despite his dissipations during this period, he played in concerts in many Italian towns. He made money and obviously did not gamble it all away, for in 1801, he offered his father the interest on a thousand pounds, a large sum of money for those days. His father refused the interest and demanded the entire sum, which Paganini gave him. It was then that Paganini turned his financial affairs over to the lawyer Germi of Genoa, who was to be his lifelong friend and adviser.

One of the now-exploded myths about Paganini is that he perfected his technique and composed his famous twenty-four caprices in Genoa during its long siege by the Austrians. He was, in fact, not in Genoa at the time, but in Lucca, though shortly after, sometime in 1801, he disappeared completely for three years.

During Paganini's lifetime and for many years afterwards, the story persisted that he had spent these three years

in prison for murder. Actually, as Paganini later explained
to a biographer, though with reluctance and discretion, the
time was spent in retreat with a titled lady in a castle in Tuscany. He never revealed the identity of the lady, who is
known to history only as Dida, the name he gave her on
music that he composed for her. Dida, whoever she was, had
a very beneficial influence upon him, and the years he spent
with her brought him to maturity. She apparently liked the
guitar and may have played it herself, for Paganini took up
the instrument during their retreat, mastered it, and composed a number of pieces for it. He later said that his study
of the guitar had extended the span of his left hand and
helped him gain his celebrated chord effects on the violin.

In 1804, Paganini returned to the world, reappearing in
Genoa, which was now French and at peace. Here, he spent
another period of intense study. He also at this time gave
lessons to one of the few pupils who later could claim to have
been taught by him. This was a fifteen-year-old violinist,
Caterina Calcagno, who later had a successful career in
Italy. Another development of this period was Paganini's experiments with and adoption of *scordatura,* the false tunings
of the violin that by then had gone completely out of fashion.

The following year, Paganini left Genoa and resumed his
career, playing first in churches at Lucca, where he so enraptured his listeners that they forgot where they were and
burst into wild applause. By this time, he had in his possession the instrument that was to be his favorite for the rest of
his life. This was a magnificent violin by Guarneri de Gesù,
which he had received as a gift, probably some years before,
from a wealthy French merchant in Leghorn, M. Livron. The
story, which Paganini never denied, though he was to deny
so many others, is that he had lost so much money at gambling that he was forced to pawn the violin he was using at
the time. Since he had to perform at a concert in Leghorn, he
was told about M. Livron and went to ask him if he could
borrow the Guarnerius. M. Livron lent him the violin, and
then, having heard Paganini's concert, refused to take it
back.

Lucca, having put itself under the protection of Napoleon, who had crowned himself Emperor of France on December 2, 1804, and a few months later was proclaimed King of Italy, took advantage of the situation to appoint as its ruler the husband of his eldest and most troublesome sister, Marianne Elise. Needless to say, Pasquale Bacciochi, who was a well-born nonentity, was to be ruler of Lucca in name only; his wife, who became the Princess Elise of Lucca and Piombino, was the true ruler. After her triumphant state entry into Lucca, on July 14, 1805, she appointed Paganini as her chief court musician. His duties required him to conduct the opera at those performances attended by the court, to play himself at court two or three times a week, and to arrange other court concerts. He also gave violin lessons to Prince Bacciochi, for which he received an extra fee.

Princess Elise was known as the ugliest of the Bonapartes. Tall and thin, she was something of a bluestocking, both intellectually and politically ambitious, and certainly intelligent. She quickly established a salon that, while it lasted, was one of the most brilliant in Europe. History can neither confirm nor deny the suggestion that she and Paganini were lovers, though it is not entirely unlikely.

Between 1805 and 1808, while at Lucca, Paganini began to affect the mannerisms that were to become part of his stock-in-trade: long hair down to the shoulders, a wide range of facial expressions, and the exaggerated pose while playing that was so often to be caricatured but which obviously was the one he had found to suit his purposes most successfully. This pose consisted of standing with his full weight on the left hip with his right leg, bent at the knee, thrust forward.

Another famous Paganini story concerns a court performance at which he presented what he called a *Scène amoureuse*. This was a musical dialogue played on two strings only (G and E) that supposedly depicted the full range of emotions experienced by two lovers. The court adored it; and Princess Elise then asked why, if he could do so much on two strings, he could not do as much on one. This gave the impetus to one of Paganini's most celebrated feats. He com-

posed a sonata that he called *Napoleon* for G string alone,
which, with other similar pieces, became standard in his
repertory. In them, he succeeded in extending the span of
the G string to three octaves.

In 1808, Paganini, who was ever to be restless, obtained
permission from Princess Elise to go on tour. His first concert, in Leghorn, was nearly a disaster. Having hurt his foot,
he came on stage limping, and the audience laughed. Next,
the candles fell out of a music stand, producing more laugh-
ter. Finally, Paganini broke a string, which got the house to
roaring. But he went on playing, doing on three strings what
was expected on four. The audience became fascinated,
calmed down, and then succumbed. The concert ended in
triumph.

Next, Paganini went to Turin, where he played before
Princess Paolina Borghese, the beautiful sister of Princess
Elise. Here he suffered a severe attack of an intestinal illness
from which he emerged with the emaciated appearance that
was to remain his for life and which became part of the
legend, adding to rather than detracting from the magnetic
effect of his person, which produced excitement and awe the
moment he appeared on a stage.

In October of 1809, Paganini was recalled by Princess
Elise, not to Lucca, but to Florence, where she wished him to
participate in the festivities surrounding her investiture as
Grand Duchess of Tuscany, a prize she had wheedled from
Napoleon, who now was at the apex of his career. In December, Paganini resumed his tour, traveling by coach from one
northern Italian city to another, arranging concerts only two
or three days in advance, and usually staying at the house of
a prominent musician or officer of the town. The tour continued for more than a year, after which his patroness insisted that it was high time he returned to her court at Florence.

By 1812, the fortunes of the Bonapartes were on the wane.
Paganini, no doubt sensing what was to come, contrived a
way to effect his dismissal by the Grand Duchess. He appeared at a concert he was to conduct wearing a uniform

instead of evening dress, as was required. The Grand Duchess ordered him to change. He refused. She ordered him again. He refused again. Then she dismissed him; and he left. Afterwards, of course, she ordered, then begged him to return. But he, suspecting that her day was almost over, did not.

Another attack of illness kept Paganini idle for some time. But on October 29, 1813, he reappeared at La Scala in Milan, performing a concerto by Kreutzer and introducing a new work of his own, *Le Streghe,* variations on a theme from the ballet *Il Noce di Benevento* by Franz Xaver Süssmayer, friend and pupil of Mozart. This concert was such an extraordinary success that Paganini gave eleven more in Milan in the next six weeks and reappeared there thirty-seven times in the next five years. He developed a great fondness for Milan, often played there at court, and in private played chamber music with other players, particularly works by Beethoven, who, more than any other composer, was his god.

In 1814, Paganini became a friend of the young composer, Gioacchino Rossini, and composed several sets of variations on themes from his operas. Seven years later in Rome, he conducted the *première* of Rossini's opera, *Mathilde de Shabron* (not one of his successes) at the Teatro Apollo, having offered to do so when the scheduled conductor became ill.

From 1814 to 1828, Paganini's life followed a pattern. Triumphant appearances in every important Italian city were interspersed with periods of intense illness. He was deeply suspicious of doctors but became addicted to patent medicines of all kinds. He once said that the only good advice he ever got from a doctor came from an American, who prescribed "plain food, good wine, fresh air, and rest."

In 1818, Paganini played at the Teatro Carignano in Turin and was the first attraction ever to fill that vast theater. In the same year at Piacenza, he met one of his nearest rivals, the Polish violinist and composer, Carl Joseph Lipinski, with whom he became good friends. Lipinski had been trying for a year to catch up with Paganini, though not, as generally was assumed, to engage him in a contest. However, the two violinists did perform together in a double concerto. Lipinski, who became celebrated for his big, powerful tone, which was the one thing in which Paganini was said to be deficient, was sometimes called a pupil of Paganini, despite the fact that he was twenty-eight when they met and already famous.

Two years before, in 1816, Paganini had had a similar encounter with another contemporary violinist of great reputation, Charles Lafont, a pupil of Kreutzer and Rode, with whom he also became friends and with whom he played a double concerto by Kreutzer. Despite all the calumnies lodged against him by musicians who never knew him, Paganini was liked by the musicians who did know him and worked with him. Even Louis Spohr, who was austere by nature and held strong views, formed a good opinion of him as a person when they met in Venice in 1816. The composer Giacomo Meyerbeer, who became a lasting friend, was so enthralled by his playing at Florence in 1819 that he followed him from city to city to hear him in eighteen concerts. Prince Metternich, the wily Austrian statesman, became friends with him in Rome in 1817 and begged him to go to Vienna, which he did not do for another eleven years.

Paganini's triumphs, from Turin to Palermo, went on and on, year after year, and as often as he was well enough to perform. He always had singers, usually recruited locally, performing with him. The solo recital was as yet unknown and undreamed of. The music that he himself performed was almost always his own. He made the decision to play the music of composers other than himself only in private quite early in his career, though from time to time he did perform a concerto by Rode or Kreutzer, to prove that he could and to quiet the rumors that for some reason or other his technical prowess was somehow dependent upon the music he composed. He was accused of not publishing his music because he was unwilling to give away his technical secrets, though more likely it was to avoid pirating and to discourage imitators. Some recent scholars have suggested that Paganini feared that his music could not stand on its own and that, as a composer, he suffered from an inferiority complex. True, he never permitted musicians to keep his music and carefully collected it and carried it away with him after every rehearsal. Also, he never gave anything more than sketchy indications of how he was going to play at rehearsals, so that orchestral musicians wondered what the excitement was all about until the actual performance, when they found out, which was one reason why the men in the orchestra often were cheering him as wildly as the audience. Some of his performances, for which he later was scorned by his detractors, featured imitations of animal noises, which enraptured audiences in less sophisticated cities. Stunts of this kind were commonplace in those days and for years afterwards; and Paganini had no objection to following fashion. In later years and in greater cities, his performances on the G string alone did for audiences what imitations of animal noises had done before.

Paganini made a great deal of money even in those days, when he played mostly in cities where admission prices customarily were lower than elsewhere. He took a large percentage of the gross at every concert. He later was accused widely of avarice and meanness, though most unjustly. He often gave all or part of the receipts of his concerts to charity and, before he had a son to provide for, was quite careless about money. His detractors did not know, because he was too proud to proclaim the fact, that he supported his family in Genoa for the rest of his life. His father died in 1817, but his beloved mother lived until 1832. His sisters married improvident men, and he had to contribute to their support. So far as playing for charity was concerned, he liked to pick and choose and act on impulse. He resented, as so many famous musicians have come to do since, the suggestion, constantly put forward, that he should play for charity every time he was asked.

The only pupil that Paganini ever acknowledged as a successor to him was brought to him in Genoa in 1823. This

was Camillo Sivori, who was then seven or eight years old
and was introduced to Paganini by his old teacher, Giacomo
Costa. Paganini gave Sivori lessons whenever he was in
Genoa over a number of years. His efforts were rewarded, for
Sivori became one of the star violinists of the next generation, touring throughout Europe and in North and South
America. Born in 1815, he appeared in public for more than
forty years, retiring in 1870, twenty-four years before his
death in 1894.

Some sources state that one of Paganini's well-known contemporaries, G. B. Polledro, was his pupil; but he was in fact
a year older than Paganini and studied with Pugnani, which
accounts for the confusion. Paganini was interested in
teaching but had little time for it. He claimed that he could
and had transformed mediocre string players into very good
ones in three days' time. He often spoke of his "secret,"
which he intended to reveal in a method. But he never did,
and we do not know what it might have been, if indeed it did
exist. Nobody yet has been able to explain "the secret of Paganini" in any terms except those of exceptional talent, the
right physical attributes, personality, unstinting labor, and
incredible endurance. It was said that after his early successes, Paganini never practiced, though he must have had
to in order to play again after one of his long illnesses. He
always played from memory, a practice almost if not completely unknown in his time. His feats of sightreading, performing any work put before him not only as written but
with intricate embellishments, were famous among musicians. Historians, at a loss to explain the fabled magic of
Paganini and finding in the scores of his concertos and other
music little to account for "the incredible beauty and profound feeling" that were attributed to his playing, failed to
take into account the fact that he nearly always improvised,
so that no two of his performances were exactly alike. The
technical feats can be explained and duplicated; but the
effect of his tone, the sometimes suffering lyricism of his
adagios, which, more than his technique, transported his listeners, are lost to us completely. His motto was *Bisogna forte*

sentire per far sentire (to make others feel, one must feel deeply).

Though his fame spread abroad rapidly after his first Milan triumphs and the publication of his twenty-four caprices, it was fifteen years before Paganini answered the constant call to perform outside Italy. By then he had formed a liaison with a singer, Antonia Bianchi, whom he first met in Venice in 1815 but did not see again until 1824. She became the singer at all of his concerts and, having been thoroughly trained by him, appears to have sung quite well. She was, however, a spitfire, bad-tempered, insanely jealous, and possessed of only the most superficial values. Her attraction, which must have been considerable, would have faded for Paganini very soon, as had that of many others, if she had not given him a son. Born in Palermo on July 23, 1825, the boy was named Achille Cyrus Alessandro, after three great conquerors.

Achillino became his father's pride and passion. When he was still very young, he fell and broke a leg. The doctors said he must not be permitted to move until the bone set. To prevent this and ease the child's restlessness, Paganini held him on his lap for an entire week, during which he did not sleep and after which he became very ill. In addition, Paganini was afflicted with a disease of the leg, in as good an example of probable psychosomatic reaction as can be found in history.

In Milan, in 1828, Paganini played a new concerto at a private concert with piano accompaniment. This was the work for which he is best known today, the Second Concerto in B Minor with the famous finale called *La Campanella*. The public *première* took place at his first concert outside Italy, in Vienna on March 29, 1828. The concert, which was given in the Redoutensaal, a ballroom of the Hofburg or imperial palace, began at noon. It started with Beethoven's *Fidelio* Overture. Then Paganini appeared, not from the wings as in most theaters, but through a door directly in the center of the wall above the orchestra. He then came down one of the two flights of stairs that descend to it. His extraordinary appearance, which by this time was macabre if not, as some said, ghoulish, created a sensation, one that was strengthened and increased by his playing of the concerto. When the excitement finally subsided, Bianchi appeared to sing an aria by Paër, Paganini's old teacher. She was politely received. Paganini then performed his *Napoleon* Sonata for G String Alone, after which Bianchi sang another aria. The concert ended with Paganini performing his Larghetto and Variations on the Rondo from Rossini's *Cenerentola*. Present at the concert were Franz Schubert, who could ill afford the raised prices but said afterwards: "Such a fellow will never come again"; Joseph Mayseder and Joseph Böhm, the leading violinists of Vienna and two of the finest teachers in Europe; and other eminent violinists of Vienna such as Leopold Jensa, Joseph Slavik, and Léon de Saint-Lubin.

Nothing before or since could be compared with Paganini's effect in Vienna. The city went wild about him. As one witty but probably disgruntled writer wrote in the *Austrian Observer*, he "temporarily dethroned the giraffe recently sent by the Pasha of Egypt." True, everything in Vienna, a very faddish city, had been *à la giraffe* but now became *à la Paganini*. Clothing, foods, cigars were named after Paganini; the violin as a motif appeared everywhere, as beauty marks, on ladies' stockings, in the shape of cookies, etc.; and men and women wore Paganini's picture on their hats or pinned to their clothing. Poems, satires, stage burlesques were written about him. Waltzes quickly were produced to Paganini tunes.

At Paganini's second concert, on April 13, the hall was full three hours before it began. Apparently, the seats were not reserved and ticket holders came early to get a good place. At a later concert in England, the hall was full seven hours before Paganini appeared.

One of Paganini's great hopes had been to commission a work from Beethoven in Vienna. But the great master had died just a year before. Paganini was heartbroken; but he did commission a piece of descriptive music called *The Storm*, which is what he had wanted from Beethoven, from an indifferent composer named Joseph Panny. This he dutifully performed at his eleventh and last concert in Vienna.

Vienna's fantastic reception either had a bad effect on Bianchi or else gave Paganini the impetus to make a break, for he and she came to the parting of the ways while they were there. Paganini gave a concert for her benefit, settled a large sum on her, permitted her to keep all the clothes and jewels he had given her, and sent her on her way back to Venice. All he kept was the music he had arranged for her, and their child.

It is hard to understand a woman who could almost literally sell her child to its father, which in effect is what Bianchi did. Paganini never saw her again. Whether or not Achillino did, we do not know. Bianchi's side of the story, and she must have had one, has not been recorded in history, and so it would not be fair to judge her now.

In Vienna, Paganini, though the idol of the public and newly created chamber virtuoso to the Emperor, was forced to deny rumors about his supposed term in prison for murder. Later, he several times wrote letters to the newspapers in an attempt to refute the stories. It has been suggested that this was simply a clever way, not of refuting them but of drawing attention to them, for the sake of the publicity. We do not know just how and when the most damaging part of the Paganini legend got started, that which concerns his supposed pact with the Devil, in which he exchanged the promise of his soul for the possession of his gifts. At one of his Vienna concerts, a man jumped to his feet and cried that he could see the Devil standing behind Paganini, directing his playing. That story and many others like it were soon being told everywhere. The Gothic tales of E. T. A. Hoffman had recently come into popularity; and in the world of fashion, ordinary superstition had taken on a literary gloss. It probably was inevitable that Paganini should be accused of diabolism. It appears to have amused him, though it must often have annoyed him, too. He probably played up to it at times, knowing it would do no harm at the box office.

After vacationing at Carlsbad with Achillino for three

months, Paganini next went to Prague, where he gave six
concerts. His reception there was somewhat different and
not so wildly successful, partly because of the advanced
prices of the tickets but also because of the intense rivalry of
Prague with Vienna. He next went to Dresden, where he
played for the court, and then to Berlin, where he was welcomed by his friend, Meyerbeer, who said: "Where our
powers of thought end, there Paganini commences." In Berlin, Paganini played in the opera house built by Frederick the
Great and was enthusiastically received by Frederick's successor, Frederick William I, who gave him the title of *Kon-
zertmeister*. Paganini's stay in Berlin was somewhat disturbed by an intense cabal against the director of the opera,
Gaspare Spontini, composer of many operas, including *La
Vestale*. Since Spontini had befriended Paganini and openly
admired him, some of the spite and resentment aimed at
Spontini fell upon him. But at Warsaw, where he played at
festivities celebrating the coronation of the Russian Czar,
Nicholas I, as King of Poland, his triumph was complete.
All of his concerts were played to capacity. He was reunited
with his friend Lipinski, who was leader of the royal orchestra. Frédéric Chopin, then just twenty, heard him in Warsaw and soon afterwards composed his piano piece, *Souvenir
de Paganini*.

At Breslau, Paganini performed between movements of
the Beethoven Fifth Symphony, which, despite his worship
of Beethoven, appears not to have disturbed him.

From 1829 to 1831, Paganini toured Germany, making
his headquarters in Frankfort and giving concerts in at least
thirty-three cities. Goethe, who was then eighty, heard him
in Weimar; the poet Heine heard him in Hamburg; and in
Kassel, he was met by Louis Spohr, who was court music
director there. Robert Schumann, who was to make transcriptions of the Paganini caprices and characterize him in
his *Carnaval*, said, after hearing him in Frankfort: "Paganini is the turning point in the history of virtuosity."

The Revolution of 1830 prevented Paganini from going to
Paris for some time. But after the dethronement of the Bour-

bon king, Charles X, and the enthronement of the "bourgeois king," Louis Philippe, Paris was itself again, and Paganini was ready to descend upon it. However, when he arrived, he was somewhat disconcerted to find that everywhere shop windows featured imaginative pictures of him in prison, and large crowds were staring in at them. If he was recognized, it happened more often than not that men and women looked down to see if he had a cloven hoof.

Because the fame that had preceded him to Paris was so great and the expectations that had been raised so high, this debut, which he was to make at the age of forty-eight, was probably the crucial event of his career. It took place at the Opéra on March 20, 1831. The composer-violinist, François Habaneck, who had tried to master the Paganini caprices and given it up, conducted the orchestra. Appearing on the program with Paganini were three popular singers from the Opéra, Adolphe Nourrit, Rosalie Levasseur, and Julie Dorus.

The strain on Paganini must have been incredible, and he was near collapse when the concert ended. But his triumph, which was of a kind that then could be achieved only in Paris, was absolute. After the concert, Baillot, the dean of French violinists and professor at the Conservatoire, said to the famous mezzo-soprano, Maria Malibran: "It is marvelous, inconceivable; do not speak to me about it—there is in his playing something that drives one to distraction."

Perhaps the person most affected by Paganini's first Paris concert was the young pianist, Franz Liszt, not yet twenty. Completely bowled over, he swore then and there that he would work to become the Paganini of the piano, which, with some help from Paganini himself, he succeeded in doing. Another musician profoundly affected by Paganini was the violinist, Heinrich Wilhelm Ernst, who followed him slavishly, attending all his concerts, and eventually became the best of his immediate successors. Also deeply affected was Habaneck's pupil, Jean Delphin Alard, an eminent violinist who, twelve years later, succeeded Baillot at the Conservatoire.

Paganini swept away all memories of his rival contempo-

raries in Paris, particularly that of Alexandre Boucher, who
until then had been considered brilliant, and Jean-Baptiste
Cartier, a pupil of Viotti, who was the leader of the Opéra
orchestra at the time of Paganini's debut. From eleven concerts in Paris, Paganini realized 165,000 francs. He received
a great deal of bitter criticism when he refused to play at a
charity concert but, in the following year, failed to get good
publicity when he returned to the cholera-infested city to
play a benefit for the victims of the dread disease.

It only remained for Paganini to conquer London, which
he proceeded to do at his debut at the King's Theatre on June
3, 1831. Luigi Lablache, one of the greatest singers of his
time, appeared with him. Afterwards, the pianist, Johann
Cramer ("Glorious John"), said, "Thank Heaven, I am not a
violin player."

The London of this period, which was that of the reign of
King William IV, was pleasure-loving and gossipy and enjoy-
ing its last time of laxness before the Victorian era. Fifteen
theaters were in operation. Mrs. Siddons and Edmund Kean
had just died; but the acting profession still could boast of
Kemble and Macready. The finest singers in the world were
appearing in London, including Maria Malibran, Giuditta
Pasta, Antonio Tamburini, Luigi Lablache, and G. B. Rubini.
But Paganini outshone them all, drawing capacity crowds to
the largest theaters, including Covent Garden.

The arbiter of all things musical in London at this time
was the Bohemian pianist, Ignaz Moscheles, known as "the
prince of pianists." His memoirs are a valuable record of the
musical life of the period. A proper, courtly man, cautious
but not ungenerous, he was fascinated by Paganini but
deeply suspicious of him. They once played the Beethoven
Kreutzer Sonata together in private. Moscheles, who had
known Beethoven, was horrified by Paganini's interpreta-
tion. Paganini, though he revered Beethoven above all
others, may, as a matter of course, have provided embellishments and otherwise indulged in departures from the letter
of the score. He was supremely himself and probably
could not avoid imposing his style on everything he played.

Conservative musicians like Moscheles, having been told that Paganini was a charlatan, were inclined to believe it, for he was not a conservative musician and never had lived like one. The same thing was to happen with Liszt. Even today, musical snobs approach Paganini and Liszt with condescension. But the twenty-four caprices, which were composed early in Paganini's life, though ostensibly intended as an exhibition of the most advanced technique, reveal an awareness of the musical values of the classical Italian school, with sophisticated echoes of Vivaldi, Tartini, and Veracini. Thus, it might be concluded that Paganini, despite his individual gifts and the intensely romantic aura surrounding him, was essentially a classicist, but with a difference peculiarly his own.

The high prices that Paganini charged caused some trouble in certain English towns, particularly Brighton, and he was forced to lower them. In Leeds, he played to the biggest take of his career and gave some of it to charity. In ten months, he gave 140 concerts in England, Ireland, and Scotland.

After returning to Paris in 1833, Paganini was much berated for refusing to play at a benefit for Harriet Smithson, the Irish actress whose Shakespearean company had just failed. The composer Berlioz, who was about to marry Miss Smithson, did not hold a grudge and was glad to accept from Paganini a commission to compose a viola concerto. Paganini had heard a performance of Berlioz's *Symphonie fantastique* and been swept away by it.

For some reason, perhaps to do with the country's newly achieved independence, Paganini was received with hositility in Belgium, where he was careful never to return. He then returned to England, where, being now familiar, he was less of a sensation. Still, he gave a great many concerts and made a lot of money. At this time, he became involved in a scandal involving a young lady whom he had thought had musical talent and wished to encourage. Her father, an avaricious and disreputable man, took him to court. The young lady, a Miss Watson, later toured America and advertised herself as "the ex-fiancée of Paganini."

In Paris again, Paganini found himself less popular. He also declined to play the concerto Berlioz had composed for him, the *Harold in Italy*, on the grounds that in the viola solos there was not enough for him to do.

By this time, Paganini was suffering from the illness that was to prove fatal, an inflammation of the larynx that made it almost impossible for him to speak. It was called tuberculosis but probably was cancer. By now, he had satisfied one of his greatest desires, which was less for himself than for his son, when he was raised to the nobility. The King of Westphalia had made him an hereditary baron.

In 1834, Paganini returned to Italy. He visited Genoa and, in order to have a lordly seat to go with his title, purchased an estate near Parma, the Villa Gaione. He gave his first public performance in six years in Italy at a charity concert in Piacenza. At the end of the year, he played at a birthday party for Napoleon's widow, Marie Louise, who was now the Duchess of Parma. He was at this time very much concerned in litigation to legitimatize Achillino, an effort in which he at last succeeded. After playing in a concert at Nice, which then was part of Italy, he appeared again, and for the last time in public, at a concert in Turin on July 9, 1837.

His terrible affliction had made Paganini remote and often morose. He could speak to people only through Achillino, who was able to understand the croaking noises that were all Paganini had left of speech. In 1837, he was further depressed by the failure of a gambling casino in Paris with which he had been involved, having promised to give it his name and to perform there regularly, which he was unable to do. Lawsuits following the failure resulted in a loss to Paganini of 60,000 francs.

The next year, on December 16, 1838, he heard the concert at which Berlioz's *Harold in Italy* had its *première*. Afterwards, he appeared before Berlioz, who was surrounded by important people on the stage, and, kneeling, kissed his hand. This gesture became the talk of Paris, as Paganini knew it would. Berlioz, who was in severe financial straits and suffering from ill health, profited much from this, as he did from the 20,000 francs that Paganini sent him the next day. So great was his reputation for avarice and parsimoniousness, however, that Paganini was refused the credit for this generous gesture. The story persisted for years that he was acting as agent for somebody else, who wished to remain anonymous. Even Jeffrey Pulver, who in 1936 published the biography of Paganini that finally did justice to him, accepted this explanation. But since then, scholars such as Jacques Barzun have recognized it as having no basis and have come to the conclusion that Paganini, overcome by admiration for a great and original talent, did what he did entirely on his own initiative. The grateful Berlioz dedicated to Paganini his next important work, the *Romeo and Juliet* Symphony, which, unfortunately, Paganini never heard, though he did see the score.

Paganini's dramatic gesture toward Berlioz was his last act as a public figure, for soon afterwards he left Paris to seek a warmer climate. Returning to Genoa after a stay in Marseilles, he again met his pupil, Sivori, and presented to him a copy of his Guarnerius de Gesù that had been made for him in Paris by the firm of Vuillaume.

The last weeks of Paganini's life were spent at Nice, where he slowly sank into darkness, attended by his faithful Achillino. Three days before his death, a priest came to give him the last rites but was dismissed by Paganini, who probably did not want to think he was nearing the end. Just before he breathed his last, on May 27, 1840, he reached out to take hold of his violin, the Guarnerius de Gesù that had served him faithfully for forty-three years.

The grisly story of what happened to Paganini's remains can be told briefly. Since he had died unconfessed, he was denied Christian burial by the Bishop of Nice, who thought it more significant that Paganini in his will had forbidden any composer to write a requiem for him than that he had asked for the Capuchins to say a hundred Masses for the repose of his soul. One version of the story holds that Paganini did not dismiss the priest who came to confess him but had been denied absolution by him unless he would confess his pact with the Devil. Another version, given by Paganini's housekeeper, modifies the story by claiming that the priest merely made a joke ("This is hardly the time to be scraping your fiddle") at which Paganini took offense. However it was, the refusal of Christian burial in a Catholic country in those times was a serious matter and created serious problems. Paganini's coffin was first placed in a building at Villafranca, from which it soon had to be removed because of the protests of superstitious villagers. Next, it was placed in the wall of an olive-oil factory, but seepage of the oil made it necessary to move it again. Finally, four years after his death, Paganini was granted Christian burial, thanks to the unrelenting efforts of Achillino, now Baron Paganini, who had launched numerous lawsuits. Buried first near Genoa, the body next was transferred to the courtyard of Paganini's estate, the Villa Gaione. In 1876, there was a reburial in the Parma cemetery. After a further reinterment in 1896, when the cemetery was moved to another location, the city of Genoa finally claimed her illustrious native son in 1926, when his remains were removed to the Camposanto there.

Among Paganini's possessions at his death were seven Stradivari instruments, including two cellos and a viola, an Amati violin, and several Guarneri in addition to the Guarnerius de Gesù. A Stradivarius was bequeathed to Sivori and the Guarnerius de Gesù to the city of Genoa, where it was to be kept in the municipal museum. However, Achillino could not bear to part with it; and the city did not get possession of it until 1851, when he finally was forced by law to give it up.

Paganini provided for his sisters in his will and also for Bianchi. But the bulk of his fortune, which for those times was a large one, went to Achillino. The most important collection of Paganiniana, including papers, music, instruments, and personal possessions, is in the Hayer Collection in Cologne.

After Paganini's death, and even before, a great deal was

written about him, most of it more false than true. He became immortalized, however grotesquely, in plays, novels,
operas, operettas, and ballets. But he created no school and
had no real successors, though people claimed that Ernst
and Sivori, both superb violinists, did capture some of his
style. Many others claimed the same for themselves, of
course, but without any basis of justification.

Violinists are still fond of playing Paganini's caprices and
concertos, which serve as splendid showpieces. They have
great interest from the standpoint of technique and a certain
melodic charm. But as a composer, he had more in common
with the school of Viotti and Cherubini than with Mozart or
Beethoven. To hear his compositions as they sounded in
Paganini's hands remains a possibility that probably never
will be realized, for whatever qualities made him unique
could not be put down on paper or taught to another. There
was then no phonograph to capture them; and they now
exist only as part—the true and essential part—of the Paganini legend.

Paganini probably always will live in legend and, though
but fitfully, in his music. In the future, he will probably live
on—somewhat ironically—mainly in the piano transcriptions of Liszt and Schumann and the piano variations of
Brahms and Rachmaninoff. Even advanced contemporary
composers are not above turning to Paganini, as witnessed
by the recent orchestral variations by Boris Blacher and the
two-piano variations of Witold Lutoslawski. The late Alfredo
Casella composed a tribute in 1942 that he called *Paganiniana.*

The most recent return of Paganini in his diabolic guise
was in Michel Fokine's ballet, *Paganini,* set to the Rachmaninoff *Rhapsody,* popular in the 1940's. Since then, the real
man has been permitted to emerge. Now not a single book
about him is currently in print. Perhaps, after more than a
hundred years, the tumult and shouting finally have died.

12

Louis Spohr

1784—1859

Though he was but two years younger, Louis Spohr outlived the fabulous Paganini by almost twenty years, which
meant that, while he was basically a classicist who wor-
shiped Mozart and did not always approve of Beethoven, he
was to feel the impact of romanticism and even, at the end
of his life, serve as one of Richard Wagner's earliest advo-
cates.

Spohr was a fortunate man. He won patronage and wide
fame early and kept them during a long life. His music, now
largely neglected, was universally admired and respected in
his own time. Though he held strong views, he was person-
ally generous and worked hard to promote the works of
others, even some that he did not happen to like. History has
rendered the verdict that he was one of the best of second-
rate composers, a judgment that neither he nor the majority
of his contemporaries could have suspected, for he often was
hailed as the greatest living composer at a time when Chopin, Berlioz, Liszt, and Schumann were producing some of
their best works and Franz Schubert, long dead, was almost
forgotten.

Since Spohr and his admirers were passionate supporters of all things Germanic, particularly in music, and were greatly influenced by a kind of heavy intellectualism that came in the wake of Goethe, Schiller, Hegel, and Kant—eminent philosophers of their own and the previous generation —they could not be expected to take seriously the operas of Rossini, Bellini, Donizetti, and the early Verdi, which in our time have supplanted the operas of Spohr, Cherubini, Spontini, Meyerbeer, and others who held firmly to the classical line.

Though Spohr was christened Ludwig, he was always known as Louis. His birthplace usually is given as Brunswick; but he appears to have been born in the home of his maternal grandfather, a Lutheran clergyman, at Woltershausen, near Hildesheim, which is not far from Brunswick and was at the time in the province of its duke. The date was April 1, 1784.

Spohr's father, a physician, was a self-made man, having run away from home in his teens. He played the flute. Spohr's mother was a good singer and pianist. Soon after his birth, his parents moved to the nearby town of Seesen, where four more sons and one daughter were born to them.

It has often been pointed out that extraordinary precocity in children generally manifests itself only in three fields, those of music, mathematics, and chess. The young Spohr early conformed to this pattern by displaying exceptional ability both as a musician and as a chess player. His father was not pleased at the idea of his becoming a professional musician, since it promised nothing but a precarious life and brought with it no social advancement or distinction. Still, being himself musical, he gave the boy training and submitted gracefully when his future direction became obvious. Happily, both Spohr's father and mother lived to great ages and spent many years basking in his fame.

In 1790, Spohr started lessons at Seesen with a M. Dufour, with whom he performed his first composition, a duet for violins. The following year, M. Dufour advised more advanced study; and the seven-year-old Spohr was sent to

board with a baker's family at Brunswick, where he began
training with a violinist of the ducal orchestra named
Maucourt. Soon afterwards, he played at his first public concert.

With a large family and a practice that was hardly lucrative, the elder Spohr had limited resources. So, when his son
was fourteen, he sent him to Hamburg to seek his fortune,
giving him a small amount of money. Poor Spohr was so
frightened by his first experience of a large city that he
quickly left. He then had the good idea of presenting himself
to the Duke of Brunswick and asking for his patronage.

In those days, Germany was made up of some three hundred independent states, most of them sovereignties but
some of them ecclesiastical enclaves. There were also a few
free cities, such as Hamburg and Bremen, which were relics
of the Hanseatic League, established in 1239 and once a
powerful union that extended to eighty-five towns. The
League was one of the casualties of the Thirty Years War
(1618–48). The fact that young Spohr could simply walk
into the palace garden and approach the Duke of Brunswick
while he was taking a stroll indicates that rulers of some
small states were readily accessible to their subjects.

Fortunately, the Duke of Brunswick was not a high-
handed autocrat but a kindly, culture-loving man. Spohr's
good fortune began with him, for the Duke quickly appointed him to his orchestra, which was a fairly good one. It
was while playing in the ducal orchestra that Spohr formed
his passionate attachment to the music of Mozart.

The Duke of Brunswick soon became aware that in Spohr
he had a protégé with extraordinary talents. He offered to
send him to any teacher he chose, wherever he was. Spohr
decided he wanted most to study with Viotti, then living in
London. But Viotti, in answering his letter of application,
said that he no longer took pupils, being too much occupied
with the wine trade. Spohr next applied to Ferdinand Eck,
concertmaster of the court orchestra at Munich. But Eck,
about to move to Paris, declined and recommended his
brother, Franz, who was touring in Germany. Franz Eck was

brought to Brunswick and began training Spohr rigorously.

Before long, Eck had an offer to go to Russia. The generous Duke thought it would be good for Spohr to go there with his teacher, so that he could continue his lessons and, at the same time, see something of the world. Eck and Spohr went first to Hamburg, where they had contacts with the famous Bohemian pianist, Jan Ladislas Dussek, then slowly worked their way to Russia. Spohr composed his first violin concerto on the way, during a protracted stay at Strelitz.

Arriving in St. Petersburg in the dead of winter, the travelers found their activities hampered by the cold and snow, with the result that Eck concentrated on Spohr's training. However, Eck managed to secure the appointment of director of the court concerts; and Spohr had to return to Brunswick without him. Though Eck obviously had been a superb teacher, Spohr was not too sad to leave him, having discovered him to be a man of less than the highest character. Spohr, of course, was very young then and easily shocked; but he was always to be an idealist and the most proper sort of man.

In Russia, Spohr earned the admiration of a violinist named Remy, who, when they parted, insisted that they exchange violins as a token of friendship. Since Remy's violin was a fine Guarnerius and Spohr's an indifferent instrument, he tried to refuse. But Remy, who must have been incredibly generous and probably recognized Spohr as a far superior player, would not take no for an answer. Before leaving Russia, Spohr also had the experience of hearing the violinist who then was considered the finest in the country but who had gone insane and stopped playing. For some reason, he suddenly began to play again, though not for long. Spohr in his autobiography gives the man's name only as Crazy Tietz. He also described his meetings in St. Petersburg with the pianist and piano manufacturer, Muzio Clementi, and his young apprentice, John Field, who was to spend his adult life in Russia. Spohr first met Field in a freezing piano warehouse and saw nothing but an awkward boy in clothes that were too small for him. But when he sat down to play on piano keys that were coated with ice, Spohr, young as he was, recognized a genius.

When Spohr returned to Germany, he found a country much changed by the Napoleonic conquests. One hundred and twelve German states had been dissolved and ninety-seven ceded to France. But the peoples of the southern and central German states tended to hate the Prussians more than the French. Fortunately for Spohr, the Duke of Brunswick, though humiliated by Napoleon, was permitted to continue as ruler of his small state.

In June, 1803, the violinist Pierre Rode, one of the masters of the French school, came to Brunswick. He was then at the height of his powers, and Spohr was deeply impressed by his playing. His own playing was always to be modeled on the French school; and he considered Viotti and Rode, rather than Paganini, the true masters.

Soon after hearing Rode, Spohr played his own concerto with the court orchestra for the Duke of Brunswick and achieved such a success that the good Duke appointed him to the position of first violin, a great distinction for a youth of nineteen. In January, 1804, the Duke gave him permission to go on tour, together with a cellist named Benecke. They intended to go as far as Paris; but the Napoleonic wars prevented them. The theft of his precious Guarnerius, from a trunk strapped to the back of their coach, was a great blow to Spohr; and it was years before he was able to acquire an instrument of comparable quality.

In Leipzig, Spohr was asked to play at a private party. He chose to play an early Beethoven quartet with three local musicians. It is significant that he always referred to the other players in a quartet as "accompanists," for later critics were to remark that his chamber music, of which he composed a great amount, always revealed undue emphasis on the role of the first violin. At that time, a Beethoven quartet was esoteric fare. The guests at the Leipzig party soon grew restless and very talkative. Spohr stopped playing and refused to continue. The host suggested that if he would only play something less difficult, the response would be more to his liking. So he switched to a piece by Rode, to which the guests paid proper attention. Thus began Spohr's long campaign for quiet and attention at his concerts, which gradually succeeded but caused him sometimes to be disliked. No one, except possibly musicians, then thought of music as anything but a diversion, to be listened to or not as one wished. Even at public concerts and in opera houses, people moved about or chatted during the music. In later years, when romanticism took hold, the public—which meant the aristocracy and the bourgeoisie that imitated it in all things —was not content simply to listen. It became the fashion for ladies to swoon in ecstasy and for men to sigh deeply and loudly.

Despite this early discouragement, Spohr continued to campaign for Beethoven, who was then still a struggling composer, although he met much resistance, such as that from one princely host who asked him, "Why do you play that baroque rubbish?"

In Dresden, Spohr became attracted to a young singer, Rosa Alberghi, with whom he performed. She apparently expected him to marry her, and Spohr's parents hoped that he would. But Spohr married someone else, and the disappointed Rosa eventually entered a convent.

Spohr was rapidly making his name in Germany. In 1805, he was invited to become concertmaster to the court of Gotha. The Duke of Brunswick encouraged him to accept the post. After leaving Brunswick, Spohr went to visit his friend Dussek at Magdeburg, where he was much in the company of Dussek's patron, the dashing and very musical Prince Louis Ferdinand, nephew of Frederick the Great. The following year, the Prince was killed at the battle of Saalfeld; and Spohr's benefactor, the Duke of Brunswick, who had become commander of the Prussian armies, died of wounds received at the battle of Jena.

At Gotha, Spohr found things much to his liking. The orchestra was good; and since only one concert a week was required, there was plenty of time for rehearsals. One of the permanent court singers was Madame Scheidler, whose

daughter, Dorette, aged eighteen, was a talented harpist.
Spohr soon fell in love with Dorette. The entire court ap-
proved; and the two were married in the ducal chapel on
February 2, 1806.

Dorette was also a good violinist; but Spohr considered the
violin an unsuitable instrument for women, and she gave it
up. However, Spohr began composing works for the harp,
including the Fantasy, op. 35 and the Variations, op. 36,
which still attract harpists, who do not have such a large
repertory that they can afford to ignore them. He also composed for the harp and violin together and discovered that a
brilliant effect was achieved by tuning the harp a semitone
below the violin.

While the Napoleonic wars were raging and, as a result,
Germany was feeling the birth pangs of nationalism, Spohr,
blissfully unpolitical, was busy preparing concerts and composing violin concertos and an opera that was never produced. His first daughter, Emilie, was born in May of 1807.
Soon afterwards, he and Dorette went on tour. They played
for Goethe at Weimar and before the rulers of Bavaria and
Würtemburg, who had been made kings by Napoleon. At
Stuttgart, Spohr, who had heard that the court played cards
during concerts, demanded that they not do so while he and
his wife were playing. This was agreed to; but the King got
even by not applauding, which meant that nobody did, since
applause was permitted only if led by the King.

It was at Stuttgart that Spohr first met Carl Maria von
Weber, a composer of whom he did not have a very good
opinion but who joined with him in his campaign for more
respectful attention to music and more respect for musicians. Weber also shared with Spohr the distinction of being
one of the first real conductors, as distinct from leaders, who
gave their cues from the pianoforte or, if they were violinists,
with the bow. Spohr later claimed to be the first to use a
baton; undoubtedly he was the first to do so in England.
Weber, Berlioz, and François Habaneck are others who were
among the first real conductors.

A *Concertante* for two violins that Spohr composed and

which he often performed with his pupil Hildenbrendt became the favorite work of the Duchess at Gotha. But another opera, in which Goethe was interested and which was submitted to him at Weimar, failed to find a production. In September, 1808, Spohr was at the congress of German princes at Erfurt and managed to get into a performance by the French troupe Napoleon had brought from Paris by bribing a horn player, who let him take his place in the orchestra. Spohr managed to master the horn well enough in one day to get away with the substitution. The following year, he was presented to Napoleon at Gotha, and while on another tour with Dorette, played for Jerome Bonaparte, the new King of Westphalia, at Breslau. Dorette had given him another daughter, Ida, the year before.

The Spohrs became very popular in Germany. Dorette was much admired as a harpist, and Spohr was considered to be the finest violinist in the country, rivaled only by Andreas Romberg, who was seven years his senior. Romberg, who later succeeded Spohr at Gotha, had flurried Paris in 1784 and then settled in Hamburg, where he produced a number of operas. He and Spohr met in Hamburg and played quartets together. After Romberg's death in 1821, Spohr reigned as leading violinist in Germany for some years, though he was increasingly more occupied with composing and conducting.

In 1810, Spohr led the first German music festival at Frankenhausen, which featured a hundred singers and more than a hundred instrumentalists. Haydn's *The Creation* was given and several works by Spohr, including a double concerto and a clarinet concerto. The next year, the festival featured the first performance of his First Symphony. In 1812, he composed his first oratorio, *The Last Judgment,* for a festival at Erfurt in celebration of Napoleon's birthday. This marked the beginning of his involvement with large choral works, which soon were to become the fashion again, and, in preparation, he made an intense study of counterpoint and learned much from the manual on the fugue by Friedrich Wilhelm Marpurg.

In the same year, 1812, the Spohrs made their first trip to Vienna. Finding that Rode was about to give a concert, Spohr hurriedly arranged one at an earlier date. He enjoyed a definite success and was called by a local critic "the nightingale among all violin players." Rode attended the concert. His own, a few days later, was a failure, for he was by this time well past his prime. Later, at a private party, Spohr played a piece of Rode's that the master had played himself at his concert, thereby calling attention to the fact that he could play it much better than Rode could by this time. Poor Rode was hurt; and Spohr afterwards criticized himself severely for his thoughtlessness.

Spohr's oratorio was given in Vienna and was conducted by Antonio Salieri, the leader of the Viennese musical establishment who held or eventually would hold all the important posts. Though the Viennese disliked his oratorio, Spohr was offered the post of leader at the Theater an der Wien. Since Vienna was one of the musical centers of the world, the Theater an der Wien one of its important theaters, and the salary offered three times what he received at Gotha, he accepted. The Duke and Duchess of Gotha were offended. Spohr, when he went home alone to fetch his children, had to face their displeasure. However, he was able to take with him from Gotha his brother and his friend and pupil, Moritz Hauptman, both of whom he engaged for the orchestra of the Theater an der Wien. He was also hopeful of producing an opera in Vienna, which he had not been able to do at Gotha; but the one he composed, a version of *Faust* that was not set to Goethe's play but to another text, was turned down by the patron of the Theater an der Wien, Count Palffy, with whom Spohr was to come into conflict. Still, *Faust* was not composed in vain, for it eventually was produced, and with some success, by Giacomo Meyerbeer in Berlin.

In Vienna, Spohr met and became friends with Beethoven. He played in benefit concerts under the master's direction and left touching accounts of his conducting, which, because of his deafness, usually was either ahead of or behind the orchestra. Musical historians set Spohr down as being an opponent of Beethoven's music, which was not the case. He was critical of some of it, particularly the Ninth Symphony, which he eventually was to conduct at Kassel. Spohr merely regarded Beethoven as a contemporary whom he was free to judge according to his lights, which, in those days, were strictly classical and held only Mozart sacred.

The rise of the bourgeoisie and their interest in music as a status symbol was exemplified by Spohr's unusual arrangement with a patron, Herr von Tolst, who paid him a large sum for the exclusive rights for three years to all the works he composed in Vienna. One of these works was the Nonet in F, op. 31, one of Spohr's most enduring compositions. In the end, Herr von Tolst ran into financial difficulties and had to cancel his contract with Spohr. By that time, Spohr was disenchanted with his post at the Theater an der Wien, having found himself too much hampered by the management. Herr von Tolst was forgiven, particularly when Spohr sold all of the works committed to him to two Viennese publishers.

During his brief return to Gotha, Spohr had encountered the ragged armies of Napoleon retreating from the Russian winter after the disastrous invasion of 1812. Now, he found himself in Vienna during the glittering congress that was to determine the fate of nations but was temporarily prevented from doing so when Napoleon escaped from Elba. The Spohrs gave two concerts during the congress, and Spohr conducted others, including one that featured his cantata in celebration of the liberation of Germany. Another outstanding musician of the period, the young pianist, Ignaz Moscheles, made his reputation during the congress, and other concerts were given by such luminaries as the pianist J. N. Hummel and Beethoven himself. Spohr played under Beethoven in a performance of the master's Seventh Symphony and wrote about it admiringly.

After resigning his post in Vienna, Spohr gave a farewell concert at which he played the *première* of his Seventh Violin Concerto, a rousing success. He left Vienna with a great reputation and, in his music album, a canon specially composed for it by Beethoven himself; Weber was producing his

Faust in Prague; a musical prince had invited him and his family to summer with him at his estate in Silesia; and he had decided to satisfy a strong ambition by making a tour of Italy.

Spohr and Dorette did not go to Italy for another year; first they toured Germany again and then took a summer vacation in Switzerland. To prepare for his venture into Italy, Spohr composed a new concerto that he modeled after the *scena* and *aria* of Italian opera. This was a canny move on his part, for the Eighth Concerto, known as the *Gesangscene,* proved very popular in Italy and is one of the two concertos by Spohr still sometimes played today.

The Italian tour began in Milan, where Spohr played the *première* of his *Gesangscene* at La Scala on September 9, 1816. Though he was competing with Paganini, now the idol of Italy, he was well received. The Italians were flattered by the *Gesangscene.* Dorette, too, was admired, for her looks as well as her playing. In the long run, the tour proved to be only mildly successful and failed to earn much money for the Spohrs, who at first were shocked by the dirt and poverty of Italy and the behavior of Italian audiences, but slowly succumbed to the country. They even spoke of one day settling in Naples. In Venice, Spohr conducted the Beethoven Second Symphony, thus earning the admiration of Paganini, who was there at the time. The two violinists met; but Paganini politely declined Spohr's request that he play for him. It was to be fourteen years later that Spohr finally heard him. In Florence, Rossini's *L'Italiana in Algeri* was being given. Spohr heard it but disliked it, though he later, without much modifying his opinion, was to produce several Rossini operas at Kassel. In Naples, the new San Carlo opera house, one of the largest in Europe, was opened while Spohr was there; and he was invited by the impresario, Domenico Barbaja, to play solos during the intervals. He did so somewhat nervously but was pleased to find that his tone carried well in the huge theater.

Upon their return to Germany, the Spohrs found a changed atmosphere. Reform was in the air, soon to be followed by oppressive counter-reform. The new nationalism was expressed in a fashion for folk music and the sudden rise of large choral societies and men's choruses (called *Liedertafeln*). Spohr quickly composed a four-part song for male chorus to a poem by Goethe. He and Dorette played in Cologne, Düsseldorf, and several cities of the Netherlands before settling in Frankfort, where he had been appointed director of opera and music. Here again, he came into conflict with the management, which was very cautious and pennypinching. As a result, he resigned after two years. However, he did produce an opera of his own at Frankfort, *Zémire und Azor*, which, strange to say, had more than a few touches borrowed from Rossini.

Upon leaving Frankfort, the Spohrs made another tour, beginning in September, 1819. In Brussels, they met Alexandre Boucher, a violinist of some brilliance who had a resemblance to Napoleon that he had exploited to the full but now regretted. He also toured with a harpist wife. Spohr was astonished to discover that Boucher permitted his wife to tune her own harp, a task he himself always performed for Dorette.

Arriving at Calais, Spohr found, on the day they were scheduled to make the crossing, that the English Channel was very rough and, because of Dorette's fear of the sea, postponed the trip for one day. The ship they would have taken was lost and driven to the Spanish coast, thereby giving rise to the rumor that the Spohrs had drowned. This caused their families in Germany much anguish until the news arrived that they were safe in England.

In London, Spohr made his debut with the Philharmonic Society, playing his *Gesangscene*. Among those who applauded him was Viotti, the master with whom he had wanted to study. At a later concert for her benefit at the Argyll Rooms, Dorette played the harp for the last time in public. She had adopted the new, heavier Érard model but had found it too much for her strength. She then turned to the piano; and she and Spohr played together in this more conventional combination.

On their way back to Germany, the Spohrs traveled for the first time on the newly established railroad. After more concerts in Germany, they finally attempted the conquest of Paris.

Unfortunately, so far as Paris was concerned, Spohr was more of a success in private than in public. He played the *première* of his Ninth Violin Concerto at the Opéra, having engaged but half the evening to save money. The other half was given over to the Opéra ballet. A certain anti-Germanism was reflected by the public and critics; and Spohr may have been punished for refusing to court the critics, which it then was the custom to do. However, he was sanctioned by the all-powerful Cherubini, on whom he dutifully called. Soon, he was meeting the musical society of Paris at the house of Rodolphe Kreutzer. He and Dorette were admired for their playing of the new Piano Quintet Spohr had composed, though Dorette gave up playing it soon afterwards when she heard it performed by Ignaz Moscheles. Spohr's Nonet also became admired in various Paris salons.

The music played in private houses, whether by professionals or amateurs, still kept to a certain standard. It was sometimes advanced and sometimes reactionary, depending on the tastes of the hosts or hostesses. Chamber music was very little played in public. Later in the century, as more and more people studied music, concert life expanded, and professionals no longer gave so generously of themselves at private functions; now the kind of light, easy music that became known as salon music came into demand.

Spohr heard several of his rival contemporary violinists in Paris and decreed the best of them to be Charles Lafont, three years older than he and a pupil of Kreutzer and Rode.

In 1821, the Spohrs found themselves in Dresden, where they were thinking of settling. Here Carl Maria von Weber had been *Kapellmeister* since 1816. Now, however, he had come suddenly to great fame as a result of the production, the year before in Berlin, of his revolutionary opera, *Der Freischütz*. This work, which swept Europe and established the romantic German opera, must have unsettled Spohr, who hitherto had not thought much of Weber. It was in production by Weber at Dresden when Spohr arrived. He attended the rehearsals. Soon afterwards, Weber told him that he had received an offer to become *Kapellmeister* to the Elector of Hesse at Kassel but intended to refuse. He suggested that he could recommend Spohr, if he was interested. Spohr agreed, and negotiations began. Since a new and splendid opera house had just been built at Kassel, the post was attractive. Spohr held out for a good salary, an appointment for life, and six or eight weeks of absence every year. The Elector, Wilhelm II, who had just succeeded to the title, agreed.

So began the long association of Spohr with Kassel, where he was to live for the rest of his life. The first operas that he gave there were his own *Zémire und Azor* and Weber's *Der Freischütz*. He was to give fifty or sixty operas a year, perform at and conduct court concerts and public concerts, and organize and conduct a large choral society. His most successful opera, *Jessondra*, was first given for the Elector's birthday on July 28, 1823. This was Spohr's answer to *Der Freischütz*. Though in classical form, it had a romantic story involving an Indian heroine in love with a Portuguese explorer who is expected to commit suttee on her elderly husband's funeral pyre but doesn't. Influenced, consciously or unconsciously, by Weber, it was a genuine if not permanent contribution to the advancement of German opera. It was a great success throughout Central Europe and persisted as such to the end of Spohr's life. Today, the opera is remembered, if at all, as the work that inspired Meyerbeer's last opera, *L'Africaine*. Some critics have professed to having heard in its chromatic love music intimations of Wagner's *Tristan und Isolde*, a work composed forty years later.

Though Felix Mendelssohn gets all the credit for reviving the almost completely forgotten choral works of Bach, Spohr should get some of it, for he made several attempts to give the *St. Matthew Passion*, which the Elector found religiously objectionable, before he finally was allowed to perform it in 1832. He also deserves credit for inspiring composers to return to a German style, having published a manifesto on the subject in 1823.

In Germany and, to a lesser extent, in England, the opera was very much a court affair and available to the general public only in certain larger cities. The oratorio became the medium of the middle classes. Spohr was aware of this and turned away from opera and toward oratorio. He had adopted liberal political views, which grew stronger as the years progressed and the aristocrats tried to save their positions by suppressing liberty.

Whatever Spohr eventually thought of Weber, he produced his last two operas, *Euryanthe* and *Oberon*, at Kassel. He also produced some of Rossini's later and more serious operas and others by Meyerbeer, Méhul, Auber, Spontini, etc. His oratorio, *Die Letzen Dinge*, first produced at Kassel in 1826 on Good Friday, was given at the first Rhenish Music Festival in May of that year and was so successful that it had to be given a second time. Spohr's daughter, Emilie, was one of the soloists, performing as a last-minute replacement. Both she and her sister, Ida, were trained singers and later sang in their father's works. A third daughter, Therèse, died suddenly while still in her teens.

Spohr produced another opera of his own, *Pietro von Abano*, in 1827, but without success. He conducted the Beethoven Ninth Symphony on Easter Monday, 1828, a year after the master's death. In January, 1830, Paganini came to Kassel to play two concerts. He and Spohr spent a pleasant day together. After finally hearing Paganini, Spohr described his playing as "a strange mixture of consummate genius, childishness, and lack of taste."

Relations with the Elector were not always easy for Spohr. The court was strangely divided, as the Electress, who was very popular with the people of Hesse, lived apart from the Elector, though under the same roof. The Elector flaunted a mistress, whom he had created a Countess. Spohr sometimes was embarrassed by the necessity to serve both households. However, by 1831, the people of Hesse had forced the Elector to give them a constitution. Spohr composed a hymn to celebrate it. Soon the Elector retired with his mistress to Hanau; and the Electress and her son remained at Kassel as co-regents.

Also in 1831, Spohr published his valuable *Violinschule*, which is still familiar to teachers and students. It established the German school of violin playing. In November, Spohr's parents celebrated their golden wedding anniversary, for which he composed a cantata that was sung by members of the large Spohr family.

By this time, Spohr's classicism was disguised but not concealed by chromaticism. Otherwise, he was not much affected by the new romanticism. The vogue for program music, for music that, while not exactly descriptive, had an intellectual air about it, did not leave him unaffected, however. He began giving high-sounding names to instrumental works, such as his symphony of 1834, which he called *Die Weihe der Töne* (The Consecration of Sound).

In October of 1834, Spohr first met Mendelssohn when he came to Kassel to visit Moritz Hauptman, who was a member of Spohr's orchestra, as he had been in Vienna. The following month, Dorette died, having long been in failing health. Her devoted husband was griefstricken.

Spohr was naturally an optimist. Nothing had ever happened to him before the death of his wife that could dislodge his supreme self-confidence. Tall and massive, impressive and gentlemanly, he attracted almost everybody. Hardworking and organized, he had little time or use for the lesser details of daily living. Such a man, if he is to continue as before, must have a wife; so, a little more than a year after the death of Dorette, he was married again, to the sister of his friend, the poet Pfeiffer. Twenty years younger than Spohr, Marianne Pfeiffer was an excellent pianist and an excellent person. The second marriage was as good as the first.

Since Spohr by now had become something of a public institution, pupils came to him from near and far, even some from America. He went on composing for the violin, producing many duets to play with pupils, some of which are still of interest. He also composed four double quartets and even a double symphony. This last work, his Seventh Symphony, was given the title *Irdisches und Göttliches im Menschenleben* (The Earthly and Divine in Human Life).

In 1837, Spohr and Marianne went to Vienna, Prague, and Munich for productions of *Jessondra*, which he conducted. He heard Johann Strauss in Vienna but was unaffected by the waltz craze. In 1838, after the death of his youngest daughter, he went to Leipzig, where he met Robert Schumann. In 1839, he went again to England, where his oratorio, *Calvary*, given over the opposition of the clergy, was a sensational success. From this time, Spohr became a revered figure in England. In 1842, his oratorio, *The Fall of Babylon*, was the great event of the Norwich Festival. Spohr was unable to conduct; his patron had refused him permission to go.

Music festivals now were popular; and Spohr's music became the feature of many of them. In 1848, he, perhaps unknowingly, moved into the avant-garde when he produced at Kassel Richard Wagner's *The Flying Dutchman*, a work that he found strange but to which he was strongly drawn. He wanted to produce Wagner's next opera, *Tannhäuser*, too, but, because his patron had heard that it was shocking, was not permitted to do so until 1853.

Spohr's efforts to produce Wagner's *Lohengrin*, which its composer was frantically promoting from his exile in Switzerland, came to nothing, since the co-regents of Hesse were not willing to support the work of a dangerous liberal who had been banished from Dresden for revolutionary activities. It finally fell to Liszt to give *Lohengrin* its *première*, which took place at Weimar in 1850.

In 1846, Spohr and Wagner met at Leipzig and got on well, since they shared liberal sympathies. Spohr also visited Mendelssohn, who died the next year. The leader of the Gewandhaus Orchestra at Leipzig was a pupil of Spohr and his friend, Moritz Hauptman. This was Ferdinand David, a notable violinist, who had had the distinction of playing the world *première* of the Mendelssohn Violin Concerto with the Gewandhaus Orchestra on March 13, 1845. The Danish composer, Niels W. Gade, conducted. Mendelssohn had sought David's advice while composing the concerto and dedicated it to him. The instrument on which David played was a Guarnerius that later became known as the "David"; it is now played by Jascha Heifetz.

Spohr went again to England in 1847. His Eighth Symphony, commissioned by the London Philharmonic Society, was performed by them. His Sixth Symphony, which had been a success in England, is a strange work. Spohr called it the *Historical* Symphony, for its first movement was in the style of Bach and Handel, the second in that of Mozart, the third after Beethoven, and the fourth in Spohr's own style. Certain critics of the time commented that it was a shame that the fourth movement was the least effective. Spohr's last symphony, the Ninth, op. 143, was called *Die Jahreszeiten* (The Seasons).

The uprisings of 1848, which, so far as Germany was concerned, marked the end of the Biedermeier period and of what Sir Donald Tovey, in commenting on Spohr's music, called "a pseudo-classical period," even reached Kassel, a relatively unimportant town. There were riots in the streets. The German princes, jealous of their power and determined against all reforms, became heavily oppressive. The liberal spirit was forced underground. Spohr's relations with his patron, who shared in the panic felt by the German princes, became difficult. However, he composed in a steady stream and, whenever he could, visited other cities, where he was lavishly feted. He returned several times to England for productions of his operas *Faust* and *Jessondra,* though he had to miss the second because the *première* was delayed. On June 25, 1853, he was present at the first London performance of Berlioz's *Benvenuto Cellini,* which the composer conducted in the presence of Queen Victoria. It was a total disaster.

Spohr, who had played before Queen Victoria and been summoned to her box, was one of her favorite composers. He also was the favorite, with Mendelssohn, of the great English choral festivals. His reception in England in 1853 was the opposite of Berlioz's. He was cheered wherever he went, sere-

naded by singing societies, pelted with rose petals, presented
with laurel wreaths, and honored by concerts made up of his
works. For the rest of his life, he received similar receptions
wherever he went. However, in Kassel, he continued to have
difficulties with the co-regent, who, when he became the
Elector in 1857, finally dismissed him with a pension.
Though this was in violation of his contract, Spohr decided
to accept it. He made his farewell on November 22, conducting his own *Jessondra.* A few weeks later, he broke an arm,
ending his career as a violinist.

A few triumphs remained. When his *The Last Judgment*
was given in Würtzburg, people lined the streets and bared
their heads when he passed. There were similar demonstra-
tions in Prague and other cities.

Spohr's powers failed him in the last months of his life.
After so active and productive an existence, he was much
depressed by his inability to compose. But he was attended
by a devoted family. He died at the age of seventy-five, on
October 22, 1859. The whole of Kassel went to his funeral.
All the musicians of the court followed him to his grave; and
the Elector stood at a window with head bared as the procession passed.

The Stradivarius that Spohr purchased in 1822 from the
prominent woman violinist, Regina Strinasacchi, he left to
his pupil, August Klompel. At the end of his life, Spohr esti-
mated that he had taught 187 pupils at Kassel.

Though Spohr's music pales beside that of many of his
contemporaries, it can still give pleasure. Some of it will always interest violinists. Perhaps his happy and successful
life made Spohr overconfident and overprolific. He had a
knack for presenting conservative music in such a way that
it appeared to be newer and more different than it was; and
he pleased his listeners by suggesting profundity without actually taxing them with it. But he was, above all else, a great
craftsman and a true professional, and as such he has a permanent if minor place in the history of music.

13

Ole Bull

1810–1880

———◁———

Whether or not Ole Bull deserved to be known as "the Paganini of the North" is an argument that never can be settled. But it now seems uncontestable that, so far as audience reaction was concerned, he, more than any other, was the great Italian's heir.

Born in the Norwegian fjord country, at Bergen, on February 5, 1810, Ole Bornemann Bull was the oldest of the ten children of Storm Bull, a well-to-do apothecary. Although thoroughly Norwegian by this time, the Bull family originally was Scottish. The most musical of Ole Bull's relatives was an uncle, Jens, who was a competent dilettante and took the talented boy's part against his father. Storm Bull considered that a musical career was unthinkable. However, he did permit his son to take violin lessons at an early age from a local musician named Paulsen. When he was eight, the boy startled his family by taking Paulsen's place during a musical soirée at his uncle's house and playing through the first violin part in a quartet without any difficulty. Paulsen, it seems, was a drinker and had been too deep in wine that night to play. Soon afterwards, Paulsen disappeared from

Bergen. Since there was no other violin teacher in town, Bull
went without lessons for three years, until a Swedish musician named Lindholm moved there.

Despite the fact that Bull made great progress under Lindholm's supervision, he was, in 1828, packed off to the University of Christiana (now Oslo) to study theology. Before a
year was out, the university authorities had disqualified him
for theology and put him in charge of the university orchestra. Soon afterwards, however, there was a student rebellion
in which he became involved, with the result that he left the
University. It is not clear whether he went voluntarily or
under duress. Since his thoughts were still fixed on music
and on the violin in particular, he journeyed to the German
city of Kassel, in Hesse, to present himself to the famous
violinist and court *Kapellmeister*, Louis Spohr. Presumably,
though he was very short of money, he hoped that Spohr
would take him as a pupil. We do not know why Spohr failed
to take an interest, though it probably was because Bull's
general musical training was sketchy at best. When Bull expressed a desire to hear him play, Spohr rather grandly said
that he would have to travel to Nordhausen, where Spohr
was to make an appearance, if that was what he wanted.
Bull went but was not impressed. He thought the music and
its performance was much too dispassionate and decidedly
not to his taste. So he returned to Norway and went his own
way.

After playing in his first public concerts at the Norwegian
towns of Bergen and Trondheim, Bull managed to make his
way to Paris, where he intended to familiarize himself with
the methods of François de Sales Baillot, Charles de Bériot,
and Paganini, who was then making his Paris debut. But
when he applied for admission to the Paris Conservatoire,
where he hoped to study with Baillot, Bull was refused. The
director of the Conservatoire, Luigi Cherubini, though himself of Italian birth, was enforcing a policy that barred for-
eigners. A few years earlier, the young Franz Liszt had been
barred for the same reason.

Bull had a hard time in Paris. He fell ill and was cared for by a French woman who saw in him a resemblance to her lost son. He later married her daughter, Felicie Villeminot. However, he did hear Paganini, who did not disappoint him, and set about studying his methods and imitating him. But his was a personality very different from Paganini's. He was twenty and Paganini almost fifty. He was a powerfully built Norseman, and Paganini a sickly Italian. Paganini suggested magic and mystery with diabolic overtones; Bull's aura was of the fresh air and a sturdy peasantry with, perhaps, a suggestion of something connected with primitive gods.

Success in Paris came to Bull in a strange way. He met a certain M. Lacour who had invented a varnish that he was convinced could transform an ordinary violin into one as good as those of the Cremona masters. Bull believed that the varnish did have a beneficial effect and agreed to demonstrate the results at concerts in private houses. According to the story Bull later told, he was playing one evening in an overheated house and the varnish of M. Lacour, which recently had been applied to the violin he was using, began to melt. Embarrassed, he began to play with wild abandon, to distract himself and his listeners from the evil smell. Suddenly, his audience was spellbound. The word spread quickly. Since that season, which marked the advent of Paganini, had been one for the violin in the musical world of Paris, rumors of a young violinist with similar qualities were seized upon. Bull was engaged for a public concert, which was given on April 18, 1832. He shared the program with another violinist who was compared to Paganini, Heinrich Wilhelm Ernst, and with a young pianist who had arrived in Paris the year before, Frédéric Chopin.

Thus encouraged, Bull did what musicians generally considered practical after a successful Paris debut, which was to go on tour. He played first in Switzerland and then went to Italy. Securing an engagement at La Scala in Milan, he was a success with the audience but was criticized in print for his lack of style. Discovering that his critic was a well-known voice teacher, he presented himself to the man and for six months studied singing with him. It was to this training that

Bull attributed his *cantabile,* one of the features of his playing that was to be much admired.

This was the time when the art of *bel canto* was reaching
its zenith. The best operas of Rossini, Donizetti, and Bellini
were being produced. Bellini's *Norma* had been given its
première at La Scala just a few months before Bull appeared
there. Instrumental musicians studied the methods of great
singers, hoping to achieve the kind of *legato* that was characteristic of *bel canto.* Chopin was greatly influenced by the
exquisite melodic lines of Bellini. The young Anton Rubinstein struggled to reproduce on the piano the *portamento*
and *messa di voce* effects of the sensational tenor, G. B. Rubini. And it was probably in imitation of singers that violinists gradually developed *vibrato,* not as a special effect but as
a characteristic of tone. It was the Belgian violinist, Lambert
Massart, who was a year younger than Ole Bull, that made
vibrato a feature of the style of the Belgian school of violin
playing, which, later in the century, was to become dominant. During these years, the rage for the operas of Rossini,
Donizetti, Bellini, and Meyerbeer was so intense that every
instrumental concert had to consist of transcriptions, fantasias, or potpourris based on arias from them. Paganini had
anticipated this vogue with his brilliant display pieces based
on themes from Rossini's early operas. It was this fashion,
more than anything else, that delayed the general acceptance of Beethoven's music. In Germany and to some extent
in England, serious instrumental music was able to hold its
own against the pervasive influence of *bel canto;* but in
France and Italy, and even in Vienna, audiences, for a time,
would listen to nothing else.

Bull's next great success was at Bologna, where he appeared as a last-minute replacement for the Belgian violinist,
Charles de Bériot, and the celebrated opera star, Maria Malibran, who was soon to marry de Bériot.

Successes followed in Venice and Florence, where Bull
composed his *Polacca guerrera,* which was to serve as the
pièce de résistance at his concerts for years to come. At Naples, he lost his best violin, which, years later, he recognized

in the collection of a Russian nobleman. After playing in
Rome in February, 1836, he returned to Paris. Here, he played
a concert at the Opéra, after which he was praised in the
Journal des Débats by the very influential critic, Jules Janin.
Having established his reputation, Bull went to England,
where, even though he was following in the wake of Paganini, he gained wide success. In two years he played at 274
concerts and made a good deal of money. In 1839, he finally
met Paganini, who had but a year more to live. In 1840, he
appeared at a concert of the Philharmonic Society in London
with Liszt, who dubbed him "Paganini's mighty rival." They
played the Beethoven *Kreutzer* Sonata. Bull, who usually
shied away from Beethoven, later played the same sonata
with Felix Mendelssohn. Like Paganini, Bull specialized in
playing his own works, at least in public, though he usually
featured something by Paganini himself, which, after the
great Italian was gone, helped further the notion that he was
his only successor. Actually, Bull, who undoubtedly had
been stung by his rejection at the hands of Louis Spohr,
identified with Paganini completely and turned his back on
the classical school. His favorite composer was Mozart,
whose sonatas he sometimes played at concerts. He also occasionally performed a concerto by Nardini, Rode, or even
Spohr. But his reputation was made playing his own pieces,
some of which, though of slight musical worth, were cleverly
composed to exploit his strengths as a player. Some others
had a simple melodic appeal, reminiscent of and sometimes
derived from folksong.

After returning to Scandinavia for a very successful tour,
Bull sailed for America, where he had been persuaded to go
by the famous dancer, Fanny Elssler. He made his debut in
New York at the Park Theater in lower Manhattan on November 23, 1843. He performed Paginini's Variations on *Nel
cor più non mi sento* and his own Concerto in A and *Polacca
guerrera*. During the concerto, a string snapped; but he went
on playing, *à la Paganini,* on the remaining three. The effect
was sensational. No doubt, Bull was accused, as Paganini
had been, of contriving to break a string, which was non-

sense. Gut strings were always snapping; and until the time when steel strings were adopted, a broken string was a common occurrence. Most players, of course, lacking the improvising skills of Paganini and Bull, had to go off and get another string before they could go on playing.

Bull arrived in America when the development of the country had reached a point where its people were ready to give their attention to cultural matters. A newly settled middle class had money to spend on them. European influences, once frowned upon except in cities like New Orleans and Charleston, were now in fashion. Music had been freed from the severity of religious restrictions and Puritan disapproval. Though there had always been musical activity in American homes, public concerts had been slow to develop. Theaters still carried the stigma of immorality; but ladies, if properly escorted, could now go to them, though concerts were considered more proper. Opera, having an aura of culture, was becoming one of the preoccupations of fashionable society. The first opera troupe in America had been that of the tenor Manuel García and his family, which opened at the Park Theater in 1825 and introduced operas of Mozart and Rossini to America. The New York Philharmonic Society came into existence the year before Bull's arrival. The first concert was given at the Apollo Rooms on lower Broadway on December 7, 1842. The leader was the violinist Ureli Corelli Hill. Only a few concerts were given each year at this time. Though musical life had been more sophisticated in Charleston, New Orleans, and even in Boston, New York rapidly was becoming the center of it in America.

Ole Bull was the first foreign musician to become a national sensation in America. There, where Paganini had never been, he had the effect of Paganini. He was, in several ways, a pioneer. The spread of the railroads made it possible for him to tour extensively and to give many concerts in a relatively short period of time. He brought music to many towns that had never heard a professional musician of great talent before. In two years, he gave more than 200 concerts, traveled some 50,000 hours on trains, and made approximately $400,000, of which he gave $92,000 to charity. His appeal was to the common people, and he became a hero to them. His strong physique, gracious and unpretentious manner, and basic simplicity, combined with an obvious superiority, made him a man whom people could admire and with whom they could also identify.

Even though this was early in America's musical history, Bull's triumph did not go unchallenged. In New York, where there was a large French population, partisans of the French violinist Alexandre Artot, who had arrived a few months earlier, claimed that he was superior and Bull a charlatan. A month after Bull's debut, a more formidable opponent arrived, the great violinist, Henri Vieuxtemps. Though probably a superior musician and certainly a better composer, Vieuxtemps's appeal was to the minority of cultivated music lovers.

The fact remains that Bull was, and still is, a legend in America. As such he takes his place beside Jenny Lind, who came to America to tour for P. T. Barnum seven years later, and Anton Rubinstein, who in 1872 revealed to the country the wonders of true pianistic virtuosity.

Having conquered America east of the Mississippi and journeyed afield as far as Cuba, Bull returned to his family in Paris. He next toured in France, Algeria, and Spain, where he played for the Queen, Isabel II, with whom, it was whispered, his relations were more than friendly Then his passionate patriotism called him back to Norway. From 1848 to 1852, he busied himself with founding and trying to manage the first Norwegian theater in Bergen. Since Norway was then under Swedish rule, the nationalist spirit was strong but embattled. Bull ran into many difficulties and, finally, when the government denied him a subsidy for his theater, turned it over to others, having by that time spent most of his fortune on it. It was at Bull's theater in Bergen that the playwright, Henrik Ibsen, got his first experience of the stage. According to some biographers, Bull was the model for Ibsen's Peer Gynt.

In 1852, Bull returned to America, where he remained for

five years. Though he again toured widely and repeated his
successes, his chief concern was with a Utopian project that
he had conceived and which he was determined to imple-
ment. Having always been conscious of the poverty of some
of his countrymen, he decided to establish a colony in America. He purchased 125,000 acres in Potter County, Pennsylvania, later acquiring 12,000 more. Settlers came from farther south in America; being from Norway, they had
suffered from too warm a climate in the south. Two hundred
houses were built, a hotel, and a church, as well as a small
house for Bull that became known as Ole Bull's Castle. The
money for all this came from Bull; and he poured more and
more into the project, money that he raised on concert tours.
In 1855, he managed an opera season at the New York
Academy of Music. The season was a failure and cost him
more money. Finally, he journeyed by ship (and by land
across Panama) to California for a concert tour, accompanied by the impresario Moritz Strakosch and a vocal prodigy, then eight or nine years old. This was Adelina Patti, who
later became one of the greatest opera stars of her time.

Returning from California, Bull discovered that the deed
for the land on which he had built his colony (named Oleana in his honor) was a false one and that he had been de-
frauded by his manager. The shock was so great and the
lawsuits that followed so trying that he lost his health. He
was aggrieved further by the rancor and bitterness of the
Oleana settlers and the public in general. Ruined financially,
he had to go on playing, though at times he was so feeble
that he had to be helped on and off the stage.

In 1857, Bull returned to his home near Bergen, where,
after gradually regaining his health, he again became involved in the management of his theater. But after a year, he
withdrew in favor of Bjørnstjerne Bjørnson, the playwright
and novelist, who was just beginning his career. He then left
Norway again and began another concert tour, performing
triumphantly in Hamburg, Vienna, Budapest, and Berlin. He
gave seventeen concerts in Stockholm alone and then gave
sixty in England.

Bull's wife died in 1862. The following year, he was back in Norway and became involved in another idealistic enterprise, which was to establish a music academy in Christiana. Failing in this, and again in need of money, he then spent three years in Poland and Russia, where he earned more than $100,000. After this, in 1867, he went to America again to give a tour of the West, beginning in Chicago. He almost drowned in the Ohio River when the boat he was on collided with another in the night.

In Wisconsin, Bull met a young woman named Sara Chapman Thorp, from a wealthy family, and he married her in 1868. She was many years younger and dominated by a socially ambitious mother. However, the marriage, despite mother-in-law trouble and several enforced separations, was a happy one. Bull had a son, Alexander, from his first marriage, and a daughter, Olea, was born of the second. After his second marriage, Bull usually followed a pattern of touring in America during the winters and returning to his home near Bergen for the summers.

In 1874, Bull enjoyed new successes in France and Italy, particularly in Florence, where people shouted that he was "Paganini risen from the dead." In 1875, he gave a tour of Norway, playing in towns all the way to the North Cape. In the winter of 1876, he played in Cairo and, in response to a dare by the King of Sweden, climbed to the top of the pyramid of Cheops and there played one of his most popular pieces, *Saeterjenten's Sondag,* which he then swore never to play again. In 1878, he was reunited with Liszt in Rome. Commenting on the music of Liszt's son-in-law, Richard Wagner, he said: "There is murder in that music, and something which appeals to the lowest passions. It makes honest people sick." This did not please Liszt, who was further offended later the same year in Budapest when he and Bull played the *Kreutzer* Sonata. Bull could no longer get through it and tried to put the blame on Liszt, who, though long since retired as a concert artist, was still second to none as a pianist.

In the year before he died, Bull gave another extensive

American tour, performing but one or two selections on programs with the soprano Emma Thursby. He also, at one time or another, had toured in what were called "concert parties" with the pianists Teresa Carreño and Anna Essipoff and the soprano Minnie Hauck.

The last winter of Bull's life was spent with his wife and her family in Cambridge, Massachusetts, where he became friendly with Henry Wadsworth Longfellow and Mark Twain. Bull's last public performance was on May 22, 1880, at the Central Music Hall in Chicago. The last piece he played was one of his own called *The Mountains of Norway*.

Knowing that he was dying of cancer, Bull insisted on returning to Norway. One of the several friends who sailed with him as far as England was the actor, Edwin Booth.

Just before he died at Lysøen, his house near Bergen, on August 17, 1880, Bull asked his wife to play parts of the Mozart *Requiem* on the organ.

All of Bergen watched the funeral procession that sailed from Lysøen across the fjord to the town. The hills were black with people. The composer Edvard Grieg played on Bull's organ as the procession left the house. At the cemetery, the eulogy was spoken by Bjørnson.

Some of Bull's appeal, particularly in the America of that time, can be found in the titles of some of his most popular pieces: *The Niagra, Nightingale Fantasy, Solitude of the Prairies,* and *To the Memory of Washington*.

Louis Spohr, who had been unimpressed by Bull in 1829, was present at a concert he gave in Kassel nine years later. This is what he wrote about Bull's playing: "His many-toned strokes and the accurate certainty of the left hand are remarkable, but like Paganini, he sacrifices too much to the tricks of the art. His tone on the weak strings is bad, and he can only use the A and D string on the lower part and *pianissimo*. This gives to his play a great monotony when he can not bring in his tricks of art. On the other hand, he plays with much feeling, but not with a cultivated taste."

Bull's favorite violin, which he willed to his son and is now in a museum at Bergen, was a 1742 Guarnerius de

Gesù. He also owned, but seldom used in public, two violins by the early master of Brescia, Gasparo da Salò. Another violin by another master of Brescia, Giovanni Paolo Maggini, was lost but eventually was found in Pennsylvania by Ole Bull's grandniece, the American soprano, Inez Bull. Since Bull possessed unusual strength, he used a special bow that was heavier than the standard one. His most famous technical feat was a downward run of 110 *staccato* notes in one downward stroke. He also, by using a level bridge and a flat fingerboard, could play four parts in a synchronized fashion.

As for Oleana in Pennsylvania, it is now the Ole Bull State Park. An annual music festival in honor of Ole Bull was inaugurated in Potter County in 1953.

I4

Henri Vieuxtemps

1820–1881

⌒

The French school of violin playing yielded to the Belgian in the person of Henri Vieuxtemps, who was born in Belgium in the town of Verviers on February 17, 1820. However, it was another Belgian violinist, Charles de Bériot, who effected the transition.

The son of a retired army officer who had become an instrument maker and piano tuner, Vieuxtemps received lessons from his father and then from a local teacher named Lecloux before making his debut at the age of six, playing the Fifth Concerto of Pierre Rode with an orchestra at Verviers. Then his father took him on tour. He was only eight when de Bériot heard him and adopted him as his pupil and protégé.

De Bériot, born in Louvain in 1802, was also a prodigy. A disciple of Viotti and a pupil of Baillot, he made a brilliant Paris debut at nineteen and was appointed violinist to the French King, Louis XVIII. At the time of his discovery of Vieuxtemps, he was solo violinist to the court of the Netherlands.

Vieuxtemps remained with de Bériot until 1831, when he

returned to Belgium from Paris. De Bériot went on an Italian tour with the mezzo-soprano, Maria Malibran, one of the idols of the musical world, whom he was to marry in 1836, six months before her death at the age of twenty-eight. De Bériot, conforming to the pattern of the virtuoso-composer, produced salon pieces that were popular for years, as well as several concertos that the critic, John Erskine, described as being "full of fire and fury signifying nothing."

After Vieuxtemps's father regained charge of his son, he took him on an extended tour of Germany. Fortunately, the boy was given a respite in Vienna in 1833, when he studied theory and composition with a distinguished teacher, Simon Sechter, and won the interest and friendship of Carl Czerny and Joseph Mayseder, the leading piano and violin teachers in Vienna, both of whom had been friends and associates of Beethoven. Vieuxtemps played the Beethoven Violin Concerto in Vienna, which, though composed twenty-seven years before, had seldom if ever been performed.

On June 2, 1834, the fourteen-year-old Vieuxtemps made his debut in London with the Philharmonic Society and was hailed as a new Paganini. Already, the characteristics of his style were apparent: elegance, perfect intonation, and purity and fullness of tone.

Though Vieuxtemps's father, who had two other musical sons, was anxious to push his career, he permitted him a period of further study in Paris, where he specialized in composition with Anton Reicha, who had taught Franz Liszt. When, in 1839, he resumed touring, he went to Vienna and then, in company with Adolf Henselt, official pianist to the Czar, to Poland and Russia. He played the first performance of his Concerto in F Major in Russia and then suffered an illness, the first of many that were to plague him. He soon recovered, however, and reappeared in 1840 at the Rubens Festival in Antwerp. Soon afterwards, he made a great impression with his concerto at a Conservatoire concert in Paris and with the London Philharmonic Society. Also in 1840, he played at a gala concert at which the eleven-year-old Anton Rubinstein made his Paris debut.

When Vieuxtemps went to America at the end of 1843, he was only twenty-three but already a veteran of prolonged tours on the Continent. He toured under trying circumstances in America, but he loved travel and always was restless, so that his life, with a few intervals, was to be one of constantly moving from place to place.

In America, Vieuxtemps was the darling of the French immigrés and of society, while Ole Bull conquered the people. It is not hard to see why in those days a contest between a polite young Belgian, still very young and not impressive physically, and a massive Norseman, older, showier, and less elegant in style, should end in victory for the latter. But it was probably the music that Vieuxtemps played, which was "over the heads" of the average American music lover, that made the difference, though Vieuxtemps apparently was not a "personality" in the sense that Bull and Paganini were. His admirers created publicity for all concerned by writing articles in the papers attacking Bull and praising Vieuxtemps.

After this American tour, Vieuxtemps suffered another attack of illness, brought on by strain and overwork. He took a long rest at Stuttgart and during this time composed his Concerto in A Major, which he introduced in Brussels in January, 1845. He then began touring again. Toward the end of the same year, he married a very accomplished Viennese pianist, Josephine Elder. A year later, perhaps motivated by the desire to settle down now that he was married, he accepted the distinguished post of solo violinist to the Czar of Russia, arriving in St. Petersburg in September, 1846.

The Russian Czar, Nicholas I, was hardly a progressive monarch, though he was fond of music and kept a musical court. After 1848, the year of revolutionary uprisings that shook most of the thrones of Europe, there was strong reaction in Russia. The Czar became definitely repressive and actively anti-Semitic. Musicians were automatically suspect as possible spies. The young Anton Rubinstein, returning to

Russia, had a difficult time of it at first. Vieuxtemps was one of those who helped him most by playing with him at court concerts. His endorsement of Rubinstein helped him overcome the severe anti-Semitic restrictions. In 1855, when a new Czar, Alexander II, who was a liberal, came to the throne, a new era began in Russian musical life. Rubinstein, aided by his patroness, the Grand Duchess Helena Pavlovna, began to make plans for the establishment of the St. Petersburg Conservatory, which actually came into existence only after Vieuxtemps had left Russia. The Grand Duchess Helena was also one of those responsible for persuading the Czar to emancipate the serfs, which he did in 1861.

In 1848, Vieuxtemps heard in St. Petersburg the thirteen-year-old Polish prodigy, Henri Wieniawski, whose career, though very much shorter, was to parallel his in many ways. The son of a surgeon father and a very musical mother, Wieniawski was trained at the Paris Conservatoire, where, at the age of eleven, he defeated contestants many years his senior for first prize in violin playing. His teacher was the Belgian, Lambert Massart; and it was from him that he learned the use of *vibrato,* which he was to establish throughout the musical world and in which Vieuxtemps was to become a follower. Massart, a pupil of Rodolphe Kreutzer and friend of Franz Liszt, with whom he often performed, was considered one of the finest ensemble players in Europe. At the Conservatoire, he was the teacher of many celebrated violinists and remained there until his death in 1892.

In 1852, Vieuxtemps left Russia and resumed touring. He composed more concertos and other pieces, including a *Hommage à Paganini.* Though his concertos were very popular with violinists for a century, they are less so now, being considered too grandiose for their content. The demands of the virtuoso concerto, intended for display, tended to obscure the lyricism that was his strongest point. Certainly, he had every technical resource at his command and in his concertos naturally was anxious to exploit them. The best known of these, probably, is the Concerto in A Minor, no. 5, which he introducd in Paris in 1858, the year following his second American tour, which he made with the pianist Sigismund Thalberg, Liszt's nearest rival.

Though Thalberg and Vieuxtemps usually were well received in America, they failed to create real excitement. The New Orleans-born Louis Moreau Gottschalk was a more popular pianist and Ole Bull held the franchise for violinists. It was not until Anton Rubinstein's tour in 1872 that American audiences were ready for a great pianist and for the better music of the repertory. In 1870, when Vieuxtemps gave his third and last American tour, audiences had become more sophisticated.

Vieuxtemps's teacher, Charles de Bériot, had become professor of violin at the Brussels Conservatoire in 1842, having, for patriotic reasons, declined the professorship at the Paris Conservatoire. He helped make the Brussels Conservatoire, founded in 1832, into one of the best in Europe. He taught many talented and later successful violinists until 1853, when he was forced to retire because of a paralytic stroke and approaching blindness. He was totally blind from 1858 and died in 1870. The year following his death, his pupil, Vieuxtemps, was appointed to the professorship at the Brussels Conservatoire. In 1873, he too was partially paralyzed by a stroke and forced to retire.

The last of Vieuxtemps's violin concertos, the Sixth, was first performed by the Moravian violinist, Wilma Neruda, a pupil of Leopold Jensa. She was the outstanding woman violinist of her time and unrivaled in that category until the advent of the American violinist, Maud Powell, who was thirty years younger. In 1888, Mme. Neruda married the German-English pianist and conductor, Sir Charles Hallé, founder of the Hallé Orchestra in Manchester. She made a world tour with him in 1890–91, and in 1899, after his death, toured America on her own.

Vieuxtemps, who despite his affliction, continued to travel, died in Algeria on June 6, 1881. His protégé, Henri Wieniawski, had died the year before at the age of forty-five. He had succeeded Vieuxtemps as solo violinist to the Czar of

Russia in 1860 and held the post until 1871. During this period, he was the first professor of violin at Anton Rubinstein's new St. Petersburg Conservatory. In 1867, he played one of his own violin concertos in St. Petersburg at a concert conducted by Hector Berlioz, whose music was more appreciated in Russia than ever it had been in France.

In 1872, Wieniawski accompanied Anton Rubinstein on his historic American tour. As it happened, he was overshadowed by the great pianist, receiving only half as much money and a small share of the attention. After Rubinstein returned to Europe, Wieniawski traveled to California and gave a concert tour there. In 1874, he became the successor to Vieuxtemps at the Brussels Conservatoire, remaining until 1876, when he, too, was forced by ill health to resign.

Wieniawski married an Englishwoman, Isabel Hampton. Their daughter, Lady Dean Paul, became a well-known composer of songs and chamber music under the name of Poldowski.

The two concertos of Wieniawski, which have a strong appeal because of their bravura display and Slavic color, are still popular with violin virtuosos. It may be that, in the long run, they will hold their own with the public more successfully than the concertos of Vieuxtemps. The Wieniawski *Légende,* composed in 1859, was a very successful salon piece and can still be found occasionally on recital programs.

Though Wieniawski was a Pole, he is connected with the Belgian school through his teacher, Massart, and belongs in history with de Bériot and Vieuxtemps. Another Belgian violinist, Hubert Léonard, who was born in 1819 and died in 1890, served as de Bériot's assistant and immediate successor at the Brussels Conservatoire. He later was a noted player and teacher in Paris. De Bériot's pupil, Gesù Monasterio, also became a successful virtuoso and was a strong force in the limited musical life of Spain. He was violin professor at the Madrid Conservatory and its director from 1892 to his death in 1903. The last pupil of de Bériot, who trained with him as a child, was Émile Sauret. He toured America several times, at first in company with the pianist, Teresa Carreño, to whom he was married for a time. From 1890 to his death in 1920, he was violin professor at the Royal Academy of Music in London.

The Belgian school produced virtuosos and teachers strong enough to rival those of the rising Czech and Russian schools, which, by the end of the nineteenth century, began to dominate. To this day, however, the Brussels Conservatoire has a special and deserved appeal for students who aspire to become violinists of the highest quality.

15

Joseph Joachim

1831–1907

Almost every great violinist began as a prodigy. Naturally, not every prodigy has become a great violinist. Some talents have been destroyed by exploitation, though talent is apt to be hardy and survive. It is precocity that fades with maturity. Since history does not remember the prodigies that failed to mature, we can use for examples only those that did mature. One of these, Joseph Joachim, with the help of wise parents, fine teachers, and distinguished sponsors, not only managed to survive and mature but became one of the most revered performing artists of his time.

The town of Kittsee, where Joachim was born on June 28, 1831, was then part of the Austrian empire and is now in Hungary. The Joachim family, which was of Jewish origin and contained eight children (Joachim was the seventh), moved to Pest in 1833. The Hungarian capital then was made up of twin cities, Buda and Pest, later joined as Budapest.

Joachim began violin lessons when very young. His first teacher was a violinist of the Pest Opera, Stanislas Serwaczyński, who was to teach the young Henri Wieniawski a few years later in Warsaw. Joachim's debut at the age of seven at the Pest Adelskino (March 17, 1839) attracted much attention, including that of two noble patrons, Count Franz von Brunswick and his sister, Therèse von Brunswick, to whom Beethoven dedicated his *Appassionata* Sonata. They then sent him to Vienna to study at the Conservatory. His first teachers there were Miska Hauser, a pupil of Rodolphe Kreutzer, and Georg Hellmesberger, the first of a family of celebrated violin teachers. Later, he studied with Joseph Böhm, another great teacher, who was a pupil of Pierre Rode and the teacher of Heinrich Wilhelm Ernst. Since Paganini had just died, Ernst was then probably his most successful successor. It was he who recommended to Joachim's parents and patrons that he should study with Böhm.

When he was eleven, Joachim was taken to Leipzig, where he received a general education as well as musical training. The reputation of the prodigy was already so strong that when he made his debut at Leipzig, on August 19, 1843, four days after his twelfth birthday, he appeared under the most distinguished auspices imaginable. He shared the program with one of the leading artists of the time, the singer Pauline Viardot-García, younger sister of Maria Malibran, the adored mezzo-soprano, who had died seven years before. Joachim played a rondo by Malibran's widower, Charles de Bériot, and was accompanied by Felix Mendelssohn, who took charge of his education.

Joachim's teachers in Leipzig included Moritz Hauptman, a noted theoretician, and Ferdinand David, concertmaster of the Gewandhaus Orchestra. Both men were pupils of Louis Spohr. So Joachim was trained first by descendants of the French school and then by leaders of the German school. While studying with David, he often occupied the desk beside him in the Gewandhaus Orchestra. On November 25, 1844, he made an appearance at the Gewandhaus in a *Concertante* for four violins by Ludwig Wilhelm Maurer. The other three violinists were David, Ernst, and Antonio Bazzini, another celebrated player who was a disciple of Paganini but had been converted to the German school of Spohr.

Earlier that year, Joachim had made his debut in England, appearing with the pianist Ignaz Moscheles, who was dominant in the musical life of London, on March 28 at Drury Lane. On May 27, he played the Beethoven Concerto in D with the Philharmonic Society. This was the beginning of the long association of Joachim with English concert life, for he appeared there almost annually for the rest of his life.

In 1846 at Leipzig, Louis Spohr heard Joachim play the Beethoven Concerto, a work that Vieuxtemps had revived in 1833 in Vienna but which Joachim, in the years to come, was to do most to establish in the repertory. Spohr took exception to the cadenzas Joachim provided and called them "superfluously long, very difficult and ungrateful." The same year, Franz Liszt first heard Joachim in Vienna. The following year, he was heard and admired by Hector Berlioz in Prague. These two protean composers were to play important roles in Joachim's career. In 1849, Liszt engaged him as concertmaster at Weimar. In 1850, Berlioz arranged for him to perform under his direction in Paris. In 1853 at Brunswick, he played the viola solos in Berlioz's *Harold in Italy*. The same year at Hanover, Joachim introduced his new friend, Johannes Brahms, to Berlioz, who praised the work of the young composer warmly. Brahms was then twenty and Berlioz fifty.

Though Joachim remained as concertmaster at Weimar for almost three years, he was not entirely happy there and eventually made the difficult decision to break with Liszt. At the time of his arrival at Weimar, in the summer of 1850, Liszt was busy preparing the world *première* of Richard Wagner's *Lohengrin*, which took place on August 28. The composer was unable to attend, for he was in exile in Switzerland, having participated in revolutionary activities during the uprisings of 1848.

Liszt's circle at Weimar, which at that time, included the pianist Hans von Bülow and the composer Joachim Raff, was very excited about what they called "the new music." Joachim was then very ambitious as a composer and anxious to absorb new ideas. But he was at heart a classicist and, like Brahms, was to dedicate himself to the task of making the new romanticism conform to the old classical forms. He also was much influenced by Robert Schumann, whom he had known since his early years in Leipzig. Schumann, who was now in failing health, and his wife, the pianist Clara Wieck Schumann, did not approve of Liszt. Some said that the trouble really began when Liszt dared to try to make love to Clara, a young woman whose physical attractiveness was combined with a resolutely moral character.

After hearing Joachim play at Düsseldorf in the summer of 1850, Schumann, whose talents were in severe decline and soon to be overtaken by madness, composed and dedicated to him his *Fantasie* in C Major, which Joachim first performed in 1853. Schumann was then inspired to compose for him the Violin Concerto that remained unknown and unpublished, according to the wishes of his widow, until modern times, when it finally was resurrected by the grandniece of Joachim, the violinist Yelly d'Aranyi, and later taken up by Yehudi Menuhin. Perhaps its historical interest compensates for its being a weak and disappointing work, one of the last that came from a deeply troubled mind.

When Joachim finally decided to leave Weimar, the break with Liszt was not easy. Perhaps he was encouraged to make it by Brahms, whom he first met at Weimar in 1853 when Brahms presented himself to Liszt and, despite a warm welcome, quickly withdrew.

After breaking with Liszt on the grounds that he could not accept "the new music," Joachim accepted another post, that of solo violinist at the royal chapel in Hanover. In 1859, he was promoted to *Konzertdirektor* and conducted the orchestra. During his time at Hanover, which came to an end in 1866, he often was away on tour. In 1860, he played the chamber music of Beethoven in Paris, where, even then, it still was a novelty. Berlioz, who heard these performances, was much pleased with them, for he had been a pioneer in the long struggle to achieve proper recognition for the music of Beethoven.

Friendship with Brahms and Clara Schumann, whose career he greatly aided after Schumann's death in 1856, led Joachim farther and farther away from Liszt and his followers. In 1857, he wrote to Liszt from Hanover: "Your music is entirely antagonistic to me; it contradicts everything with which the spirits of our great ones have nourished my mind from earliest youth." He did, however, before writing that strong statement, acknowledge Liszt's characteristic kindness to him.

The feud came out in the open in 1860, when Joachim, Brahms, and Clara Schumann published in the Berlin *Echo* their notorious manifesto against "the new music." Directed toward Liszt and Wagner particularly, it created a furor, though it had little real effect, except to close the ranks of those who were for and against. Liszt, who tended to forgive and forget and was willing to welcome any straggler back into the fold, finally crossed Joachim off his list. Perhaps the split would not have been irreparable and the musicians of Europe so sharply divided for years to come had not Wagner chosen to reply in an article signed with a pseudonym—and obviously aimed at Joachim—that introduced a shameful note of anti-Semitism into the controversy.

The point of view of Joachim and Clara Schumann was much affected by the fact that they were performing artists of growing popularity and prestige. Though so much of the important music for their respective instruments had been composed years before, it was only just then gaining wide acceptance with the public. Popular taste had been for opera transcriptions and bravura pieces *à la* Paganini and Liszt. Spohr was accepted while Beethoven was not. Haydn and Mozart were tolerated but hardly recognized for what they were. Bach had been revived only in the past two decades. Virtuoso performers were expected to play their own works, preferably something new. Liszt had finally established the solo recital, but programs were still expected to feature "novelties."

But all that was changing; and Joachim and Clara Schumann were doing more than their bit to help it change. A great deal of music that had been composed for private use by its composers or their patrons and not intended for a large audience was coming into the concert hall. The orchestra had grown as concert halls grew from salons or ballrooms into large auditoriums. Public concerts now served the same purpose as public museums, which had not existed until the beginning of the century. The music of the past, like the art of the past, was no longer ignored simply because it was of the past.

Sensing that audiences now were willing to listen to serious music and take it seriously, Joachim and Clara Schumann dedicated themselves to performing only that music which they considered worthy of them. They gave long programs made up of long works played in their entirety that would not have been tolerated a few years before. Joachim announced that he would never touch a piece by Paganini or Vieuxtemps, and he never did. Clara Schumann, who startled the musical world by performing long programs entirely from memory, did much to promote her husband's music and that of Brahms, who was her lifelong admirer. But she also gave her audiences large amounts of Bach, Mozart, Beethoven, Chopin, and Mendelssohn. She and Joachim often performed the violin and piano sonatas of Brahms and, in later years, his piano quartets and quintets. Joachim revived the long-neglected solo sonatas and partitas of Bach and succeeded in impressing them upon the public. Eventually, his performances of these works, difficult both to play and to listen to, became something of a ritual, particularly in England. His loftiness of purpose was evident as early as 1857, when he refused a lucrative engagement in England because the orchestra with which he was supposed to appear made a specialty of polkas.

Since Germany was on its way to becoming a united country, its music grew more serious along with its politics. Large symphonic forms and the new music drama put forth by Wagner became the chief preoccupation of composers. The star pianist or violinist needed works to perform with large orchestras. The composer who was also a virtuoso was becoming a thing of the past, though a few remained, like Vieuxtemps and Wieniawski. Brahms introduced his own First Piano Concerto, but other pianists were more successful with it. Joachim tried to cast himself as a composer-virtuoso and produced one very successful work, his *Hungarian* Concerto, which he played for the first time at Hanover on March 24, 1860. He played it often afterwards but never was able to produce another work that achieved a similar popularity. The *Hungarian* Concerto gradually faded from the repertory after Joachim's death. Today the work has a certain reputation among violinists, but few, if any, perform it. It was considered in its time the most difficult work ever composed for the violin; but today's virtuosos, who have mastered the concertos of Karol Szymanowski, Béla Bartók, and Alban Berg, probably would not think so.

In 1866, Joachim resigned his post at Hanover and moved to Berlin. Two years later, he became the first director of the Hochschule für Musik, one of the three institutions founded in 1868 by the Königliche Akademie der Kunste. He made the Hochschule into one of the leading conservatories of Europe. In his lifetime, he gave intense coaching to at least four hundred pupils. One of the first of these, who came to him while he was still at Hanover, was Leopold Auer, who was to become probably the most celebrated of all violin teachers.

During his annual visits to London, Joachim performed regularly at the Monday Popular Concerts and the Crystal Palace, as well as with the Philharmonic Society and other orchestras. In 1862, he formed a friendship with Charles Dickens. His standing in England for sixty years was that of the finest violinist of his time. The few contemporaries who could compare with him were considered inferior musicians, as were the majority of violinists of the next generation. Of the virtuosos of the previous generation, Joachim himself was an admirer of Heinrich Wilhelm Ernst, who died in 1865, but had a poor opinion of Camillo Sivori, Paganini's pupil, who lived until 1894. Of his prominent contemporaries, he thought highly of August Wilhelmj, one of his nearest rivals, who also studied with Ferdinand David, but in later years thought that he had failed to live up to his promise. Nevertheless, Wilhelmj had a brilliant career and toured throughout the world. He is probably remembered to-day chiefly for the cadenzas he composed to the Beethoven Concerto, which still are preferred by some violinists. Another contemporary, of whom Joachim probably did not approve, was a fellow Hungarian, Eduard Remenyi, who also studied with Joseph Böhm in Vienna. He had a strong technique and specialized in passionate abandon, rather in Gypsy style. His resemblance was more to Ole Bull than to Joachim, who despised tricks, whether of technique or personality, with which to woo an audience. Remenyi was for a time violinist to Queen Victoria and very popular in the many countries of the world in which he played. He died of apoplexy while playing at a concert in San Francisco in 1898.

In 1869, Joachim founded the Joachim Quartet, with which he was to play in Berlin and on many tours until 1907, the year of his death. The other players changed from time to time, but the quality of the Quartet as led by Joachim remained standard. Though the Quartet played in a wide repertory, they were most celebrated for their performances of the complete quartet cycle of Beethoven and the chamber music of Brahms, for which they pioneered. Joachim almost always appeared with the Quartet, as well as in solo performances, during his annual visits to London. Certainly, he did as much as any musician to reveal the glories of chamber music to the general public.

Joachim's marriage to the mezzo-soprano, Amalie Weiss, which took place in Hanover in 1863, apparently was not a happy one, though it lasted for twenty-one years. Mme. Joachim, who had sung successfully in opera in Vienna and Hanover, retired from the opera after their marriage. She then concentrated on *Lieder* and was one of those who popularized the songs of Schumann and Brahms. After her separation and divorce from Joachim in 1884, she was, until her death in 1899, a professor at the Klindworth-Scharwenka Conservatory in Berlin.

Joachim made a most generous gesture in 1867 when he presented his favorite violin, a Guarnerius, to Clara Schumann's youngest son, Felix (named for Mendelssohn), who showed promise as a violinist. Unfortunately, the boy died twelve years later. Joachim replaced his Guarnerius with a Stradivarius. All of the members of the Joachim Quartet played instruments by Stradivari. Joachim's Stradivarius eventually came into the possession of the modern virtuoso Mischa Elman.

The finest fruit of Joachim's close friendship with Brahms was the Violin Concerto in D, op. 77, which Brahms composed for him and dedicated to him. One of the four or five basic works of the violin concerto literature, it was composed in the year 1878. Brahms made a great show of seeking Joachim's advice about the solo part but then largely ignored it. Joachim laughingly called the work unplayable and probably had private doubts about it, as did Brahms; but he played the first performance, with Brahms conducting the Gewandhaus Orchestra, at Leipzig on New Year's Day, 1879. The cadenzas, which are those most often played today, were by Joachim, who continued to play the work for many years and brought it to its eventual popularity. It was some years before other violinists took it up.

Another composer whose works were first performed by Joachim was Antonín Dvořák, whose Sextet in A Major had its first hearing at Joachim's house in Berlin in 1878 and Quartet in E-flat the following year. At this time, Joachim suggested that Dvořák compose a concerto for him, which he did, dedicating it to Joachim, who suggested detailed corrections of the solo part. But the finished manuscript remained in Joachim's possession for two years without his making any move toward performing the concerto. Finally, when Dvořák became discouraged, he arranged for its *première* in Prague in 1883. The soloist was the young violinist, František Ondříček, who became a celebrated player. He also played the concerto at its London *première* with the Philharmonic Society in 1886.

During the exact same months that Brahms was compos-

ing his Violin Concerto in Germany, Peter Ilyich Tchaikovsky was composing his in Russia. This work, which stands
beside the concertos of Beethoven, Mendelssohn, and
Brahms, received the same harsh treatment that had been
accorded Tchaikovsky's First Piano Concerto four years
earlier. Intended for and dedicated to Leopold Auer, who
now was solo violinist to the Czar and violin professor at the
St. Petersburg Conservatory, the Concerto in D was rejected
by him as unplayable. Tchaikovsky published it; but it remained unplayed until the violinist Adolf Brodsky, about to
go on a tour outside Russia, decided to take a chance on it.
Engaged as soloist with the Vienna Philharmonic under
Hans Richter, one of the first of the great conductors,
Brodsky announced that he would play the Tchaikovsky
Concerto. Richter agreed but reminded him that nothing
new could be played by the Vienna Philharmonic unless the
men in the orchestra approved. Brodsky played the concerto
at a rehearsal; but the men decided it would be better if he
played something else. Brodsky then refused to play at all;
and Richter backed him up. So the men finally gave in; and
the Tchaikovsky Violin Concerto, perhaps the most popular
in the violinist's repertory, finally was heard on December 4,
1881. The powerful Viennese critic, Eduard Hanslick, the
supporter of Brahms and the enemy of Wagner, condemned
the concerto unconditionally. Still, Brodsky persisted; and
the world-wide popularity of the Tchaikovsky Concerto
began to take hold after he played the London *première,*
again under Richter's direction, on May 8, 1882.

Brodsky, a pupil of Joseph Hellmesberger, the son of one
of Joachim's teachers in Vienna, also studied with Ferdinand
Laub, another fine violinist, who succeeded Joachim at
Weimar and later taught at the Stern Conservatory in Berlin
and the Moscow Conservatory. In later years, Brodsky was
violin professor at the Leipzig Conservatory. The only meeting between Brahms and Tchaikovsky took place at his
house in Leipzig. He later reported that the two composers,
who could hardly have been more different, were polite to
each other but did not really get on. After leaving Leipzig,

Brodsky was for a time concertmaster under Walter Dam-
rosch of the New York Symphony. Finally, he went to England, where he was concertmaster and for a short period
conductor of the Hallé Orchestra at Manchester. From 1895
to his death in 1929, he was principal of the Royal Manchester College of Music.

The indefatigable Joachim kept up a backbreaking
schedule for the rest of his life, working both as administra-
tor and teacher at the Berlin Hochschule, playing in Berlin
both in public and in private, and touring with his Quartet,
not only to England every year but to other countries on the
Continent. It is no wonder he composed only sporadically. In
1877, he was made a doctor of music by Cambridge University. Similar degrees later were conferred on him by the
universities of Glasgow, Oxford, and Göttingen. He also received many honors and decorations from the Prussian government, which, in 1871, after Bismarck's wars against
Denmark, Austria, and France, had become the government
of all Germany under Kaiser Wilhelm I.

In 1881, Joachim became the first conductor of the new
Berlin Philharmonic Orchestra, an honor that naturally fell
to him as the leading musician of Berlin. He gave up the post
after two years, probably because conducting was not his
chief interest and he was suffering from overwork and the
strain that resulted from the breakup of his marriage. In
1883, he played the *première* of another work dedicated to
him, the Concerto no. 2 in D by Max Bruch, who later became one of his associates at the Berlin Hochschule.

Joachim's rift with his wife resulted in a coolness between
him and Brahms, who defended Mme. Joachim's side in the
matter. Though the friendship never again was what it had
been, Brahms tried his best to restore it. He made a handsome gesture by composing for Joachim the Double Concerto
for Violin and Cello, op. 102. Though he reacted to it rather
coldly, as many critics have done since, Joachim and his associate from the Quartet, the cellist Robert Hausmann,
played the *première* under Brahms' own direction at Cologne
on October 18, 1887.

After Brahms' death in 1897, a year after that of Clara Schumann, Joachim, the last survivor of either side in the war against Liszt and Wagner, strenuously promoted the music of his old friend. A notable event was the cycle of Brahms chamber music that he performed with his Quartet and distinguished soloists in London in 1906.

The *Violinschule* that Joachim prepared with his friend and biographer, the distinguished musicologist Andreas Moser, was published in 1904 and is still a standard work for violin teachers and students. His pupils, all of whom came to him as advanced players after studying with others, included some of the finest players and teachers of the next generation, men and women such as Maud Powell, Jenö Hubay, Joseph Marsick, Willy Hess, Franz von Vecsey, Henry Such, Tividor Nachez, Bronislaw Hubermann, Hans Letz, Willy Burmester, Arnold Schering, and Enrique Fernandez Arbós.

Joachim, who was Mendelssohn's protégé and had connections with such descendants of the classical school as Spohr and Ferdinand David, was one of those who served to bring the great music of the classical period out of the salon and classroom and into the concert hall. He resisted Liszt and Wagner but lived long enough to know, surely to his regret, that theirs was the music that was coming in with the tide. Before he died, he was aware of the kind of music composed by the last great romantics, such as Bruckner, Mahler, and Richard Strauss. French music he probably would not have taken seriously, even though so much of it was of the first importance. Perhaps he was pleased by the music of the young Sibelius, an avowed Brahmsian and anti-Wagnerite, whose Violin Concerto, probably the most popular work of its kind to be composed in the twentieth century, had its *première* at the Berlin Singakademie in 1905, just two years before Joachim's death. It is possible that by this time, Joachim's inflexibility had been relaxed and he realized that in order to stay alive and vital, music must always be changing.

16

Pablo de Sarasate

1844–1908

Thirteen years younger than his contemporary, Joseph Joachim, Sarasate outlived him by only one year. The two violinists were the opposite sides of the same coin; but Sarasate's side of the coin came to resemble Joachim's more and more as the years progressed.

Sarasate's and Joachim's orientations could hardly have been more different. Joachim was uncompromisingly serious, and his outlook reflected the rise of German nationalism. Sarasate had the dash and elegance of a French-educated Spaniard, with colorful overtones from Basque and Gypsy sources.

Born in Pamplona, the principal town of Navarre, on March 10, 1844, Sarasate was the son of a regimental bandmaster and amateur violinist. He was baptized Martín Mélitón de Sarasate y Navascuez. Later, he changed his Christian name to Pablo. On his mother's side, he was Basque and so inherited strong traditions from those mysterious and independent people who are native both to Spain and to France.

His father gave him his first violin lessons, after which he received more from a local teacher, José Coutier. At the age of eight, he made his debut at a concert in La Coruña, where he was received with great excitement. A wealthy patron, the Condesa Espaz y Mina, gave him an annual subsidy, which permitted his parents to take him to Madrid, where he began training with Manuel Rodriguez Saez. Soon, he was playing at the Spanish court and became a favorite of Queen Isabel II. At this point, he could easily have become badly spoiled. The fact that he did not was probably due to a sensible and careful mother. According to legend, the Queen presented him with a magnificent Stradivarius; but the truth seems to be that the child earned enough money, young as he was, to pay for the violin himself.

In 1856, when he was twelve, it was decided that Sarasate needed more advanced training and so should go to Paris to enter the Conservatoire. While on the train, just after passing the French border, his mother, who was accompanying him, was seized by a heart attack and died. Sarasate was taken into the custody of the Spanish consul at Bayonne, who discovered that the boy was in the early stages of cholera. The consul cared for him until he recovered and then arranged for him to be taken to Paris.

Sarasate's extraordinary talent was apparent immediately to the directors of the Paris Conservatoire and particularly to the distinguished professor of violin, Jean Delphin Alard, who took full charge of him and his training. Alard, the author of a valuable method, was successor to the celebrated François de Sales Baillot at the Conservatoire. A pupil of François Habaneck, who had studied with Baillot, he was a composer of many light but brilliant violin pieces that influenced Sarasate.

Alard knew that his pupil could win all the prizes available long before he permitted him to compete for the first prize of the Conservatoire, practically a guarantee of a successful career. Sarasate won it at fourteen and at fifteen was already launched as one of the outstanding virtuosos of the time. At first, he followed the pattern of Paganini and Ole

Bull, playing opera fantasias, usually of his own arrangement, and pieces, generally with a Spanish flavor, that he composed himself. Actually, he avoided pieces by Paganini because his hands were small and he had to avoid the wider reaches. This limitation had some effect on his choice of repertory and was one reason why he specialized in his own compositions. One of these, *Les Adieux,* supposedly was written after he had been rejected by the only woman that, apparently, he ever loved, Marie Lafébure-Wély, who married someone else.

Both Sarasate and his compositions were enormously successful everywhere he went, though he carefully avoided touring in Germany for many years. His style of playing and the pieces he composed were beautifully suited to each other. His four books of Spanish dances and many other pieces, such as the *Jota aragonesa, La Chasse, Jota de San Firmín, Peterneras,* and *Navarra* (for two violins) combine original melodies, popular melodies, and folk melodies of Navarre or the Basque country. He also composed pieces on Scottish and Russian airs. His most famous work, which is often performed today, is the *Ziguenerweisen* for violin and orchestra, in which the Gypsy airs are treated with the utmost charm and refinement.

Spanish culture, particularly its music, was having a great influence in France, partly as a result of Sarasate's playing and later through that of his great contemporary, the pianist and composer Isaac Albéniz. Bizet's *Carmen,* though not at first a success, was evidence of this new influence when it was produced in 1875. Sarasate and Bizet were friends. Sarasate also was intimate with Massenet, Franck, Lalo, and Saint-Saëns, French composers who, with the exception of Franck, all paid tribute to Spain in their music.

Almost constant touring took Sarasate from the Iberian peninsula to Scandinavia and from England to Russia. He gave his first tour of North and South America in 1861. After 1870, he began playing more ambitious works, probably because first-rate composers began writing them for him. Eventually, he took up the classic works of the violin

literature, which he performed with his characteristic brio
and refinement but not, it was said, with any great profundity. He was most successful in the Mendelssohn Concerto.

The first to compose works that were dedicated to and introduced by Sarasate was Camille Saint-Saëns, beginning
with the Spanish-colored *Introduction and Rondo Capric-
cioso* in 1863. This was followed by two violin concertos, the
A Major in 1868 and the better-known B Minor in 1880.
Edouard Lalo had been a talented but obscure violist and
composer up to the time that his association with Sarasate
began. The success of his Violin Concerto in F, introduced
by Sarasate in Paris in 1874, made his reputation, which
forever was secured the following year, when Sarasate
played the *première* of his *Symphonie espagnole* at the Paris
Concert populaire (February 7, 1875). This enchanting five-
movement work was perfectly fitted to the violinist's temperament and technique. Though critics have resisted it, violinists and audiences fortunately have not. Sarasate himself
supplied Lalo with the tunes for his *Rhapsodie norvégienne,*
first performed by Sarasate in 1881.

Sarasate's fondness for Scotland and Scottish airs produced his own *Airs écossais* and two other works composed
for him and which he introduced, the *Scottish Fantasy* of
Max Bruch (1884) and *Pibroch* by Alexander Mackenzie
(1889). He also introduced Mackenzie's Violin Concerto at
the Birmingham Festival of 1885.

In 1876, friends finally prevailed upon Sarasate to take
the plunge by playing in Germany. The French defeat in the
Franco-Prussian War of 1870 had stiffened attitudes and
hardened prejudices on both sides. The cause of French
music had become a matter of pride; and Sarasate was persuaded that it was his duty to convince the Germans that it
must be respected. This he finally did, but only after a poor
start in Berlin, where he was badly received and compared
unfavorably to Joachim and Wilhelmj, the leading violinists
of the time in Germany. However, he triumphed in Leipzig,
where he played with the Gewandhaus Orchestra. The musical public in Leipzig, always the most discerning in Ger-

many, was introduced to the music of Lalo and Saint-Saëns and, thanks to Sarasate's irresistible élan, decided to like it. After that, the rest of Germany capitulated.

Like Paganini, Sarasate never practiced while on tour, though he did six hours a day during his summer vacations. Every year in July, he returned to Pamplona for the fiesta of San Firmín. An *aficianado* of the bullfight, he always watched from his hotel balcony during the annual excitement when the bulls ran loose through the streets. So great was his fame and the pride his countrymen felt in him that the fiesta of San Firmín also became something of a Sarasate festival.

Though he had a great appeal to women and always kept a supply of Spanish fans to present to the many who flocked backstage to see him, Sarasate remained a bachelor. He had the airs and graces of a Spanish grandee with that reticence and reserve characteristically Spanish. One of his eccentricities concerned money. Having no faith in checking accounts, he insisted that he be paid for every concert appearance in cash, which he kept in his violin case and carried about with him. During the last seven years of his life, he owned a beautiful villa at Biarritz, where he died on September 20, 1908.

Some of Sarasate's compatriots complained, sometimes in print, that he was not a true Spaniard and had given himself over to being French. His own father took that line when Sarasate refused to return to Spain after his graduation from the Paris Conservatoire. But in those days, a musician could not have much of a career in Spain and would have to settle for a court appointment or for teaching at a conservatory, neither of which would have earned him much money. Sarasate never taught and left no pupils. But, in his own way, he served Spain very well. In his will, he left all the gifts, decorations, and other memorabilia of his career to the city of Pamplona, where there is now a Sarasate museum. His two Stradivari went to the conservatories of Paris and Madrid.

The nearest rivals to Sarasate among his close contemporaries were Joachim, Wilhelmj, and Remenyi, very different artists and hardly to be compared. Of the younger artists, two violinists of the Belgian school were of great importance: César Thomson and Eugène Ysaÿe. A year apart in age, born in 1857 and 1858, they died in the same year, 1931. Thomson studied with four great teachers of the Belgian school, Léonard, Vieuxtemps, Wieniawski, and Massart. Ysaÿe was trained by his father and by Vieuxtemps and Wieniawski. Thomson gave many successful tours and played in America in 1894–95. A work he popularized was the pleasant but now faded Violin Concerto in A by Carl Goldmark. He became a noted teacher and worked at the conservatories of Liège, Brussels, and Paris. Late in life, he taught for a time at the conservatory in Ithaca, New York.

Ysaÿe had a greater career than Thomson. A very accomplished and ambitious musician, he was known as an "intellectual" violinist and sometimes gave concerts with Ferruccio Busoni, who had the same reputation as a pianist. Fritz Kreisler called him "the greatest of all living violinists," a becoming statement from an artist twenty years younger who himself had a claim to that title.

After establishing his reputation as a soloist on many tours, including several in America, Ysaÿe formed the Ysaÿe Quartet in 1893 and with it soon achieved a prestige comparable to that of the Joachim Quartet. After 1886, he was violin professor at the Brussels Conservatory. Later in life, he became a conductor and pioneered for modern composers at his own symphony concerts in Brussels. From 1918 to 1922, he was the very successful conductor of the Cincinnati Symphony. His health failed after a leg amputation in 1929. Some of his compositions, particularly the four sonatas for unaccompanied violin, are formidable works that present great challenges to the player, challenges that contemporary virtuosos like David Oistrakh and Yehudi Menuhin are still willing and able to meet. He also composed six violin concertos and a set of variations on a theme of Paganini, as well as symphonic works and an opera.

The ever-popular Violin Sonata in A by César Franck was dedicated to Ysaÿe and first performed by him in Brussels in 1886. Another staple of the violin repertory, the *Poème* by Ernest Chausson also was dedicated to and first performed by him, at Nancy on December 27, 1896. With the Ysaÿe Quartet, he gave the first performances of the String Quartet by Vincent d'Indy (1891); the Concert for Violin, Piano, and String Quartet by Chausson (1893); the Debussy String Quartet (1893); and, with the composer at the piano, the Piano Quintet of Gabriel Fauré (1905). The remarkable Violin Sonata by Guillaume Lekeu, who died at the age of twenty-four in 1894, was first performed by Ysaÿe in Brussels in 1892.

Another violinist of the Belgian school who successfully toured the world was Ovide Musin, a pupil of Léonard. He lived in New York after 1908 and was prominent there as player and teacher until his death in 1929.

Just as the Belgian school was producing these last great exponents, the Russian school was evolving under Leopold Auer, who was to train two generations of famous violinists. His greatest pupils, Mischa Elman, Efrem Zimbalist, and Jascha Heifetz, rose to fame between 1904 and 1912. At the same time, another school, the Czech, developed under another great teacher, Otokar Ševčic, who, at various times until his death at the age of eighty-two in 1934, taught in Kiev, Prague, Vienna, and New York. He is said to have had five thousand pupils. His most famous pupil, entirely trained by him, was Jan Kubelik, an international concert star. Zimbalist studied with Ševčic as well as with Auer. Another of his pupils of a later period is Erica Morini, undoubtedly the finest woman violinist of the present time, who is fine enough not to be put in any category except that of violinist. Other Ševčic pupils who had important careers are Jaroslav Kócian, Rudolf Kolisch, František Ondříček, Marie Hall, Hugo Kortschak, Sascha Culbertson, and Zlatko Balókovic.

Both Auer and Ševčic wrote violin methods that are still influential. They were probably the two greatest forces in modern violin teaching, though Massart's methods survive at both the Brussels and Paris conservatories, while those of Joachim were taught for many years at the Juilliard School in New York by his pupil, Hans Letz. Ysaÿe and Thomson also produced successful students to carry on the traditions of the Belgian school, and another Belgian, Joseph Marsick, who studied with both Léonard and Joachim, was the highly regarded professor of violin at the Paris Conservatoire from 1892 to 1924.

America's first great violinist was a woman, Maud Powell. Born in Peru, Illinois, in 1868, she studied first with a Chicago teacher and then in Paris with Charles Dancla, a pupil of Baillot and, like him, professor of violin at the Conservatoire. Moving to Leipzig, she became the pupil of another prominent teacher, Henry Schradieck, who was concertmaster of the Gewandhaus Orchestra and professor at the Conservatory. A pupil of Léonard and Ferdinand David, he was in his last years a teacher at music schools in New York and Philadelphia.

In 1882, when Schradieck went to the Cincinnati Conservatory, Miss Powell became Joachim's pupil in Berlin. Three years later, he sponsored her debut with the Berlin Philharmonic in the G-Minor Concerto of Max Bruch. The same year, she made her American debut in New York with Theodore Thomas' Orchestra. From that time until her death in 1920, she was in constant demand as soloist with American orchestras and had the distinction of introducing to America works by several native composers, as well as the concertos of Tchaikovsky, Arensky, Dvořák, Sibelius, and Saint-Saëns (the Second Concerto). She gave many European tours, including one as soloist with Sousa's Band, toured in South Africa, and, in later years, concertized extensively with her own women's quartet and trio. Appearing as she did at a time when the suffragettes were on the march, she became an inspiration to the women of America.

17

Fritz Kreisler

1875–1962

Of all the violinists whose playing we can remember or hear on recordings, Fritz Kreisler undoubtedly was the most enduring and the most loved. Like his counterpart and some times collaborator, the pianist Paderewski, he was one of the great concert stars and box-office attractions of his time and to concert-goers in America he became synonymous with and the embodiment of his instrument. The affection and admiration he inspired lasted throughout an unusually long career and came to him not just from audiences but also from other musicians, including his nearest rivals.

Though an international artist in the broadest sense of the term, Kreisler was born and, in many ways, remained a Viennese. The son of a physician and amateur musician, he was born Friedrich Max Kreisler on February 2, 1875.

His first teachers in Vienna were his father and Jacques Auber. At the age of seven, he appeared in a concert with the soprano, Carlotta Patti, sister of the famous Adelina. At about the same time, he was admitted to the Vienna Conservatory as the youngest pupil in its history. There he studied with Joseph Hellmesberger, who belonged to the third generation of a family of violin teachers. He studied harmony in a class taught by the composer Anton Bruckner. During these years at the Conservatory, he was exposed to the playing and musicianship of Joseph Joachim, Pablo de Sarasate, and Anton Rubinstein. When he was nine, he gave a full-dress recital at the Conservatory. At age ten, he won the gold medal of the Conservatory.

Though Kreisler's father still had misgivings about a musical career for his son, the arguments in favor were so strong that he sent him to Paris for further study at the Conservatoire. There, the boy, who was only eleven, became the pupil of Lambert Massart, then the dean of violin teachers of the French and Belgian schools. Now seventy-four, Massart had taught a number of celebrated virtuosos over a long period of time, including Henri Wieniawski, Franz Ries, František Ondříček, and, more recently, two highly successful women, Camilla Urso, and Teresina Tua. Probably the most important training Kreisler received from Massart was in intensified *vibrato*, which was not yet in general use, though it was a feature of the playing of Wieniawski, Vieuxtemps, and Ysaÿe.

During his Paris years, Kreisler studied composition at the Conservatoire with Léo Delibes and often played as a substitute first violinist in the Pasdeloup Orchestra at the *Cirque d'hiver*. Members of French orchestras were not required to play at concerts provided they sent a substitute, a strange practice that persisted until very recently and one that prevented French orchestras from reaching a standard of excellence comparable to that of orchestras in other countries.

In 1887, Kreisler won the *grand prix de conservatoire*, competing against forty-two other students, all older than he. He was playing a three-quarter Amati violin, which he was delighted to exchange for a full-sized modern instrument by Gand-Bernadel, presented as part of his prize.

The immediate result of winning the prize was an American tour, which Kreisler made with the pianist Moritz Rosenthal, then twenty-six, who was a pupil of Liszt and already had a considerable reputation. Kreisler and Rosenthal did

not play together but simply shared programs, Keisler playing with an accompanist. The contract was for fifty concerts.
Kreisler, who traveled with his mother, received fifty dollars
for each appearance. He played the Mendelssohn Concerto
with orchestras in Boston and New York and in recitals usually featured pieces by Wieniawski and Vieuxtemps.

The next few years were unsettled ones for Kreisler.
Though he continued to practice and made a few appearances, he turned his attention away from music. For a while,
he studied medicine but, finding he had no stomach for it,
switched to art. Then he did army service. At nineteen, he
composed cadenzas to the Beethoven Concerto that are considered by many to be the best ever done. Finally, he applied
for a post among the second violins with the Vienna Philharmonic but was blackballed by the concertmaster, Arnold
Rosé, the brother-in-law of the composer-conductor Gustav
Mahler. During these years, Kreisler became friendly with
Johannes Brahms, who then was in the last years of his life.
Brahms' friend, the critic Eduard Hanslick, took an interest
in Kreisler and invited him to go on a cruise to Greece and
Turkey together with Joseph Hellmesberger, Kreisler's old
teacher.

After resuming his career on a Russian tour that was not
very remunerative, Kreisler secured an engagement as soloist with the Vienna Philharmonic under Hans Richter. This
was probably due to the influence of Hanslick, who was a
friend of Richter's. Kreisler played the Second Concerto of
Max Bruch. The following year, he appeared with the Berlin
Philharmonic under Arthur Nikisch in the Mendelssohn
Concerto. Eugène Ysaÿe was in the audience and led the applause. This was the beginning of a strong friendship between the two violinists. Kreisler later played several of the
Ysaÿe sonatas for unaccompanied violin, one of which was
dedicated to him.

Kreisler really became a concert star in 1900, after an
appearance with the Vienna Philharmonic in the Viotti Concerto no. 22 that created real excitement. He then toured
extensively in France, Italy, Germany, Austria, Spain, Scan-

dinavia, and England, sometimes appearing with such prominent artists as the pianists Wilhelm Backhaus and Ernö von Dohnańyi.

On December 7, 1900, Kreisler appeared in Carnegie Hall with the New York Philharmonic under Emil Paur, playing the First Concerto of Max Bruch and his own orchestration of the Tartini *Devil's Trill* Sonata. This was followed by a performance of the Bach Concerto for Two Violins with the violinist David Mannes and an appearance with the Philadelphia Orchestra playing a Vieuxtemps concerto. He later played concertos of Spohr with the Chicago Symphony.

At the time of his Chicago appearances, the violinist Jan Kubelik was the idol of that town and had just been playing there. A rivalry was whipped up between them; but Kubelik soon returned to Europe and did not play in America again until 1935.

During this tour, Kreisler also played in a trio with the pianist Josef Hofmann and the cellist Jean Gérardy, both major artists. During his long career, he was to appear with some of the greatest musicians of his time, including Paderewski, Sergei Rachmaninoff (with whom he played in concerts that became almost historic occasions), Harold Bauer, John McCormack, and Pablo Casals.

One of Kreisler's close friends was the violinist Jacques Thibaud, a pupil of Joseph Marsick at the Paris Conservatoire, where he won first prize at sixteen in 1896. One of the finest violinists of the time, he made many appearances in a celebrated trio with the pianist Alfred Cortot and the cellist Pablo Casals. He died in a plane crash in 1953.

In November, 1902, Kreisler was married to an American woman, Harriet Lies, whom he had met on shipboard. The marriage was an extraordinarily successful one. Mrs. Kreisler gave her husband the support necessary for an artist constantly on the move and always in the limelight. She became a force in the musical society of several countries and for many years was very active in the work of the Musicians' Emergency Fund. Her husband made a practice of learning a new concerto every year as an anniversary present to her.

Thus, he came to perform the concertos of Tchaikovsky, Brahms, Mozart, and many others. Historically, the most important of these anniversary presents was his performance of the *première* of the Violin Concerto, op. 61 by Edward Elgar, with the composer conducting, at Queen's Hall, London, on November 10, 1910. The Elgar Concerto, now highly esteemed by virtuosos, did not make much progress for some years, though the astonishing prodigy, Yehudi Menuhin, had a great success when he played it under Elgar's direction several years before the composer's death in 1934.

After his marriage, Kreisler began performing music of the seventeenth and eighteenth centuries which, he said, he had discovered in manuscript. His programs began to feature such pieces as a Minuet by Porpora, *Chanson Louis XII* by Couperin, and *Andantino* by the Padre Martini, all of which he supposedly found in a monastery in Avignon. There were many others to which were attached names of composers then entirely unknown to the public. It is proof of the total neglect of music of the baroque and early classical periods that Kreisler's hoax went unchallenged, even by musicologists, until 1935, when, on his sixtieth birthday, he owned up to it. He had composed all the pieces himself. Mrs. Kreisler later said he found the composers' names simply by looking in *Grove's Dictionary.*

Perhaps Kreisler found pleasure in composing music in old styles partly because it amused him to flummox the public, but, more likely, he wanted to get away from the kind of music he had composed under his own name that had become almost too popular. Like Sarasate, he had created for himself a repertory of light, graceful pieces that were natural crowd pleasers. As Sarasate used popular and folk melodies of Spain, Kreisler used some of those of his native Vienna. As a result, he was almost compelled in his recitals to give the public his *Liebesfreud, Liebeslied, Caprice viennois, Schöne Rosemarin,* or *Tambourin chinois.* Though Kreisler may have become sick to death of being associated with these pieces, it is a tribute to him and their lasting appeal that violinists today are anything but loath to perform them.

One of Kreisler's eccentricities, if such it can be called, concerned his violins. He kept changing them. At one time or another he bought and sold several Stradivari and Guarneri, as well as other instruments, including one by Daniel Parker. He was particularly fond of the Vuillaume copy of Paganini's Guarnerius de Gesù, the one that Paganini, just before his death, presented to his pupil, Camillo Sivori.

Though Kreisler continued to reign supreme among violinists of his time, he did not lack competition. Fortunately, concert life throughout the world was now such that it could accommodate many great players. The advent of recordings also helped. In fact, Kreisler's recordings sold in the millions. His recording of the Beethoven Concerto is still available commercially and can stand up to all the many others.

It was in the first decade of this century that violinists of the Russian school began to sweep the world. They were students of Leopold Auer, either in St. Petersburg or Moscow or in New York, where he taught from 1918 to his death at eighty-five in 1930. The first of the Auer pupils to enjoy a sensational success was Mischa Elman, whose Berlin debut at age twelve in 1904 made his and Auer's name known throughout the musical world. Elman began his long American career on December 10, 1908, when he played the Tchaikovsky Concerto with the Russian Symphony in New York. His chief assets were a luscious tone and occasional bursts of fire. His career continued unabated until his death in 1966.

The next sensation from Russia was Efrem Zimbalist, the son of a conductor, who equalled Elman's success in Berlin three years later at the age of seventeen. He made his American debut in the American *première* of the Concerto in A by Alexander Glazounov with the Boston Symphony, in New York on October 27, 1911. The Glazounov Concerto, along with the Tchaikovsky and one by the Russian violinist, Julius Conus, became a kind of signature work for violinists of the Auer school. Zimbalist became enormously successful, often appearing in concert with his first wife, the soprano Alma Gluck. For many years until his retirement in 1968, he was director of the Curtis Institute of Music in Philadelphia. A close friend of Fritz Kreisler, he recorded the Bach Concerto for Two Violins with him. This was said to be Kreisler's favorite among all of his recordings.

The third of the great trio of Auer pupils was Jascha Heifetz, who, in 1912, made his debut at eleven with the Berlin Philharmonic under Arthur Nikisch. His American debut in a recital at the Metropolitan Opera House in New York on October 27, 1917, was one of the sensations of the century. For beauty of tone, perfection of technique, and impeccable musicianship, Heifetz remains the model, though he has been semi-retired for some years. Modern violin technique, with its intense *vibrato* and perfection of *portamento* and *glissando*, which were unknown even to Paganini, is exemplified by Heifetz. Those who tried to compare him with Kreisler, who was a quarter-century his senior, said that he lacked his warmth. But times change and with them styles and tastes, and we no longer tend to make a cult of personalities in music.

Leopold Auer taught two generations of violinists, many of whom had successful careers. These include Toscha Seidel, Eddy Brown, Mishel Piastro, Mischa Mischakov, Paul Stassevich, Max Rosen, Kathleen Parlow, Isolde Menges, Cecilia Hansen, Alexander Hilsberg, Joseph Knitzer, and Richard Burgin. One of Auer's last pupils was Nathan Milstein, one of today's great concert stars.

The last of the great prodigies was Yehudi Menuhin, who made his debut with the San Francisco Symphony in 1924 at age seven. A pupil of a noted teacher, Louis Persinger, who had studied with Ysaÿe, he later was trained and influenced by the Rumanian violinist and composer, Georges Enesco. Menuhin's astonishing musicianship made it possible for him to give convincing and even moving performances of the concertos of Bach, Beethoven, and Brahms while still in his early teens. His transition from prodigy to mature artist was not easy, but it was accomplished after a two-year retreat. Now, thirty years later, Menuhin is one of the few great violinists of the world.

Another prodigy of the same period, also trained by Louis Persinger, was Ruggiero Ricci, who, like Menuhin, matured into a major artist. Persinger also was the teacher of another of today's great violinists, Isaac Stern.

It seems that every notable violinist who appeared during the long career of Fritz Kreisler paid tribute to him as the prince of their profession. Tributes on his seventy-fifth birthday in 1950 included many moving ones from his younger rivals. Unhappily, the almost endless succession of triumphs for Kreisler was interrupted by hostility toward him as an Austrian in World War I. He went home and served in the Austrian army; but upon his return to America in 1923, he was welcomed back with much of the old love. His career continued in many world tours and annual American tours until he was over eighty. A slight hearing defect affected his playing in later years, though not seriously. His final triumph came when he returned to the concert stage at Carnegie Hall after suffering serious injuries in a street accident. He was then over eighty. He died in New York one week short of his eighty-seventh birthday, on January 29, 1962.

Among the prominent violinists of the present time, several strains can be detected. The distinguished Hungarian, Joseph Szigeti, was trained by Jenö Hubay, a pupil of Joachim. Georges Enesco, himself a popular concert artist and a pupil of Joseph Hellmesberger and Joseph Marsick, was the teacher of Christian Ferras as well as one of Menuhin's teachers. Another Joachim pupil, Willy Hess, was the teacher of several fine contemporary violinists, including Tossy Spivakovsky and Henryk Szeryng. Szeryng also studied with Carl Flesch, another Marsick pupil. The author of several important methods and a teacher of much fame, Flesch also taught Ginette Neveu, whose brilliant career ended when she was, while still very young, killed in a plane crash in 1949. The Belgian school is best represented today by Arthur Grumiaux, who was trained at the Brussels Conservatoire. One of our most popular violinists, Zino Francescatti, can not be attached to any of the prominent schools, for he was trained entirely by his father. The Russian school has continued to produce brilliant players, particularly David and Igor Oistrakh and Leonid Kogan.

Students of music history might conclude that all the greatest composers and conductors have been pianists. This would be a mistake. Arthur Nikisch, one of the first of the great virtuoso conductors, won the violin prize at the Vienna Conservatory, where he was trained by Joseph Hellmesberger. Arturo Toscanini stepped to the podium from the first cellist's desk. Serge Koussevitzky was a double-bass player. Eugene Ormandy began as a violinist. Among composers of this century, Carl Nielsen, Edward Elgar, Jan Sibelius, Ernest Bloch, Ottorino Respighi, Zóltan Kodály, and Paul Hindemith were all trained as string players.

Violinists, even the most successful concert stars, are always anxious to perform new works. The revolutionary Violin Concerto of Alban Berg, which has become increasingly popular, was commissioned by Louis Kastner, who played the first performance in Barcelona in 1936, the year after the composer's premature death. Kastner was also associated with the Violin Concerto of Arnold Schoenberg, composed in 1936. The English violinist, Alfred Salmonds, promoted the works of Frederick Delius; Jascha Heifetz commissioned, performed, and recorded concertos by Mario Castelnuovo-Tedesco (1933), William Walton (1939), Louis Gruenberg (1944), and Erich Wolfgang Korngold (1946); Mischa Elman played and recorded the Concerto of Aram Kachaturian (1940) and played the *première* of the Concerto by Bohuslav Martinu (1943); Efrem Zimbalist was the first to play the Concerto by Samuel Barber (1941); Joseph Szigeti introduced the Concerto of Ernest Bloch (1938) and also promoted many other modern composers, including Bartók, Prokofiev, Respighi, and Charles Ives; Yehudi Menuhin did much to popularize the music of Bartók, Bloch, and Enesco and recently has worked in collaboration with the Indian sitarist, Ravi Shankar; the Polish violinist, the late Paul Kochanski, a pupil of César Thomson, was closely associated with the two fascinating concertos by his countryman, Karol Szymanowski, which he introduced in Warsaw in 1922 and 1933; the Russian violinist, Samuel Dushkin, gave recitals with Igor Stravinsky and played the first performances of his Violin Concerto (1931) and *Duo Concertante* (1932); David Oistrakh has been the first to perform the violin concertos of Prokofiev (1935) and Shostakovich (1948, 1967); Oistrakh, Joseph Fuchs, and Isaac Stern have all performed and recorded the Violin Concerto (1940) of Paul Hindemith; and Christian Ferras has promoted the Concerto of Serge Nigg (1960).

Other artists have furthered their careers by specializing in or featuring the works of certain composers. The baroque revival has resulted in the formation of several small string ensembles and chamber groups specializing in the music of that period and led by distinguished string players such as Alexander Schneider, Robert Gerle, Anshel Brusilow, Renato Fasano, Szymon Goldberg, and Antonio Janigro. In recent years, Ruggiero Ricci has become something of a Paganini specialist; Carroll Glenn has popularized the Concerto of Andrew Imbrie (1958), and Henryk Szeryng that of Benjamin Lees (1965); Anahid Ajemian is closely associated with the violin works of Alan Hohvaness; Paul Zukofsky has made a name in the modern repertory, performing works of composers such as Charles Ives, Roger Sessions, and Krzysztof Penderecki, whose *Capriccio* for violin and orchestra he introduced to America in 1968; and Gabriel Banat has given recitals to illustrate the entire range of the twentieth-century violin sonata.

A list of today's star violinists, now that Elman is dead, Zimbalist retired, and Heifetz confining himself to chamber music, hardly comes to more than a dozen: Morini, Milstein, Stern, Francescatti, Menuhin, Ricci, Oistrakh, Kogan, Szeryng, Grumiaux, Ferras, Campoli, Fuchs, Schneiderhan, Gertler. There is a gap between the established virtuosos and those coming up. It can not be said, however, that the list of outstanding young violinists includes many who are on their way to stardom. Teachers like Persinger, Hans Letz, and Ivan

Galamian have trained fine violinists by the dozen in America, but only a few become prominent soloists. At the present time, we have: from Israel, Itzhak Perlman, Shmuel Ashkenasi, and Pinchas Zuckerman; from Germany, Edith Peineman; from Italy, Pina Camirelli; from Hungary, Joanna Martzy; from Bolivia, Jaime Laredo; from Czechoslovakia, Josef Suk; from Russia, Viktor Tretyakov; from Korea, Young Uck Kim and Kyung Wha Chung; from China, Ma si-Hon; from Japan, Kenji Kobayashi and Toshiro Eto; and from America, Michael Rabin, Erick Friedman, David Nadien, James Oliver Buswell IV, Charles Castelman, and Aaron Rosand.

If a career as a concert violinist is even more difficult and fraught with frustrations than that of a concert pianist, there are compensations. A pianist, if he fails in the concert hall, has no choice except to teach. A violinist of sufficient accomplishment can play in chamber groups or find a well-paying place in one of the ever-increasing number of major symphony orchestras. Good string players are getting scarcer and scarcer. One major orchestra recently had to advertise for them in the *New York Times*. Perhaps as orchestras proliferate, the demand grows greater. In the last few years, a new source of supply for string players has been found in the Orient. Japanese, Korean, and Chinese players are becoming better and more numerous; and the orchestras of the world are looking in their direction. This can partly be explained by the liberation of the people of the East from the confinements of their own cultures and a new and vital interest in the culture of the West. Then, too, Orientals seem to have the physique, innate discipline, and single-mindedness necessary, as well as several strong teachers, such as the Japanese Hideo Saito and Shinichi Suzuki, whose methods are very controversial.

But another explanation for the scarcity of good string players may be found in the new generation's attitude toward music, particularly in America, where traditions are going by the boards. Dynamic new forces are at work; and music is going in directions that not all of us can follow.

Computer music, electronic instruments, and hard rock may or may not contain clues to the music of the future. A six-string violin is currently being promoted with music composed for it by important composers; but it is too soon to tell whether or not it will come to anything. Future virtuosos may have little resemblance to those of the past, and their instruments may be very different, too.

Today's music students and those laymen who will make up their public are now presented with a staggering musical feast, for the whole of music is available to them, thanks to radio, recordings, television, modern scholarship, and the incredibly varied activity of musical life in all the cities. Styles, schools, and methods, from the earliest times to the present day, all can easily be seen and followed. The aspiring violinist can be forgiven if he wonders how he can achieve the technique of a Paganini, the dash and elegance of a Sarasate, and the perfect seriousness of a Joachim. Even then, he is not finished, for he must then wonder if he can charm an audience as Ole Bull or Kreisler did and master a repertory that now extends from the sonatas of Corelli to the Concerto of Alban Berg.

Young violinists today are looking to the East, while their counterparts in the East are looking to the West. But the sitar and koto are more difficult to master even than their own instrument.

If it is true, as many have said, that music as we have known it now belongs to the past and should go into a museum, those who love it will not really care and those who continue in its profession still will have much to do, for museums become more popular every day.

Glossary

---

adagio Italian, from *ad* (at) and *agio* (convenience). Tempo marking for slow and graceful musical passages. Slow movements in concertos, sonatas, and symphonies came to be known as *adagios* even if not marked as such.

allegro Italian, meaning gay or lively. Tempo marking and name usually given to movements, usually the opening ones, of sonatas, symphonies, and concertos.

appoggiatura Italian, from *appoggiare* (to rest or lean). A short note or grace note that precedes an essential note of a melody and is added as an embellishment or as a transition from one essential note to another.

arpeggio Italian, from *arpeggiare* (to play the harp). A chord in which the notes are played one after the other instead of together.

basso continuo Italian, meaning, literally, continuous bass. Also known as figured bass, ground bass, or thorough bass. The harmonic underpinnings of a musical composition, which in early music was indicated by the composer and filled out, according to harmonic laws, by the harpsichord, cello, or double bass players.

bel canto Italian, meaning, literally, beautiful singing. The term was applied to the Italian operatic style of the first half of the nineteenth century.

bourdon French, the name given to a monotonous, sustained tone produced by a drone string on the violin and other stringed instruments, the drone pipe in the bagpipes, or the drone stop in the organ.

bowing   The art of drawing the bow across the string or strings, which produces the sound in the violin and other stringed instruments.

bridge   The small bar or arched piece that in stringed instruments is set on the body at right angles to the strings and raises them above it so that the vibrations will sound.

cadenza   Italian, from *cadere* (to fall). An elaborate sole passage preceding the final cadence of a vocal or instrumental composition. The performer elaborates on and embellishes the themes that have gone before. At first improvised by the performer, cadenzas eventually were written out by composers.

cantabile   Italian, from *cantare* (to sing). Name given to a melodious passage or to a style of singing or playing.

cantata   Italian, from *cantare* (to sing). A choral composition usually accompanied by instruments or orchestra.

capriccio   Italian; also known as caprice. A lively and free form instrumental piece.

castrato   Italian, from *castrare* (to castrate). A male soprano or contralto whose high voice was kept from changing by an operation. *Castrati* were greatly popular during the eighteenth century.

chamber music   Instrumental or vocal music suitable for performance in a small audience hall.

chords   From accord. Three or more notes played together in harmony.

chromaticism   Meaning, literally, the use of color. In music, the chromatic scale utilizes semitones and has thirteen notes instead of the eight notes of the diatonic scale. The gradual acceptance of the use of half steps or semitones within any given key enabled composers to "color" their music.

clarinet   A musical instrument of the wind family.

clavichord   An obsolete small keyboard instrument, one of the predecessors of the piano.

come sta   Italian, meaning, literally, as is.

concerto   A musical composition in which one or more solo instruments is featured.

concerto grosso   A grand concerto for orchestra featuring the interplay of several equal instruments.

counterpoint   One or more melodies added above or below a

melody; or two or more related melodies combined so that each retains its character.

crescendo   Italian, from *crescere* (to increase). A musical passage in which there is a gradual increase in tone, i.e., from soft to loud in varying degrees.

descant   From the Latin *cantus* (singing), meaning the upper voice, the treble or soprano. In counterpoint, the upper part or treble line.

diatonic scale   A standard major or minor scale of eight tones to the octave without chromatic deviation.

diminuendo   Italian, from *diminuire* (to diminish or decrease). The opposite of *crescendo*. A gradual decrease in tone, i.e., from loud to soft in varying degrees.

double harmonics   Two overtones produced together.

double stops   The effect produced when a string player stops two strings with his fingers simultaneously.

drone   See *bourdon*.

dynamics   A term used to indicate various aspects of playing or singing that can not or are not spelled out by the composer. These have to do with accents, intensity of tone and volume of sound, and nuances in phrasing.

extensions   Notes or combinations of notes that require the string player to stretch his hand beyond its normal span.

fantasia   An instrumental composition in free form, not adhering to any set style. Also a composition utilizing popular airs or operatic arias.

frets   In stringed instruments, the raised marks on the fingerboard, usually ridges of metal or wood, which help guide the player in stopping the strings.

fugue   From the Italian *fuga* or flight. A polyphonic composition where one or more themes are imitated and developed contrapuntally.

glissando   Italian, meaning sliding. The effect produced when rapid scales are played by a sliding movement of the finger or hand.

harmonics   Overtones produced by the strings when they are pressed lightly rather than firmly.

harpsichord   A keyboard instrument that preceded the piano. The strings are plucked by a quill or leather tangent rather than struck by hammers, as in the piano.

homophony   Greek: *homos*, the same; *phōnē*, sound. The

style of music in which one voice part dominates while the other parts accompany or support it. Based on the chord rather than counterpoint. The sonata is the most typical form of homophonic music.

legato   Italian, meaning tied. The technique of moving from one note to another smoothly and without breaks.

lute   A stringed instrument that existed in several forms, similar to the viols but sounded differently, by plucking or twanging rather than, as with the viols, by bowing.

maestro da cappella   A title given to a musician who was director of music at a church or to the chapel of a prince or king. Later the title and its French and German equivalents (*maître de chapelle* and *Kapellmeister*) was retained for directors of court music and opera.

mandolin   A type of lute with four to six strings that are sounded by plucking with a small wedge, known as a plectrum, which is held in the fingers and is made of wood, ivory, shell, or metal.

messa di voce   A vocal effect, requiring extraordinary control, in which a single sustained note is swelled from soft to loud and then diminished to soft again.

monody   Music in which a single voice, which carries the melody, dominates, as in homophony.

mordents   A type of embellishment, produced by quickly alternating a principal tone with a secondary one, usually a half step lower. There are short mordents and long ones, usually called single and double mordents.

movement   Name given to separate sections of a sonata, concerto, symphony, etc. The ultimate sonata form, which was applied to the symphony, generally consists of four movements.

octave   A musical interval of eight diatonic degrees; and the series of notes forming the unit of the modern scale.

octave leaps   A difficult feat, requiring great accuracy, in which the left hand of the string player must jump the width of an octave up or down the fingerboard.

opera buffa   The Italian form of comic opera.

opéra-comique   The French form of comic opera.

opera seria   The traditional form of opera in the seventeenth and eighteenth centuries, requiring tragic or pathetic situations and involving mythological or historical personages. The music usually consisted of a series of solo arias with very few duets or ensembles.

oratorio   A choral work without action or scenery.

partita   A set of musical variations.

pasticcio   Italian, from *pasta* (paste). A musical composition, usually a stage work, made up of parts of other works.

pianissimo   Italian, from *piano* (soft). A musical marking indicating an extremely soft tone or a passage to be played very softly.

pianoforte   Italian, meaning, literally, soft-loud. The original name of the instrument now generally known only as the piano.

pizzicato   Italian, meaning pinched. A passage in music for strings in which the player or players pluck the strings instead of bowing.

polyphony   Greek: *poly,* many; *phōnē,* sound. An earlier musical style, preceding homophony and based upon counterpoint. Two or more voices with independent but equal parts combined in harmony. The fugue is the ultimate form evolved in the polyphonic style.

portamento   Italian, from *portare* (to carry). An effect used by singers and string players: sliding from one tone to another without touching the intermediate tones, as is done in a *glissando.*

potpourri   French, meaning, literally, rotten pot. Similar to a *pasticcio* but generally applied to instrumental music. A medley or collection of various tunes.

program music   Instrumental music that supposedly tells a story or is based on a literary subject.

rondo   Originally *rondeaux,* a dance form. Traditionally, the final movement of the classical sonata. An instrumental piece in which a theme, introduced at the beginning, recurs at intervals throughout.

rubato   Italian, meaning, literally, robbed. Fluctuations or distortions of tempo, in which the player or conductor increases or decreases the speed in one place and compensates for it in another.

scherzo   Italian, meaning, literally, a jest. A musical passage or separate composition, usually in triple rhythm and generally of a humorous character.

scordatura   Italian, meaning, literally, not in accord. Special or false tunings of a stringed instrument, used for special effects.

solo   Italian, meaning, literally, alone. A piece of music intended for performance by one person with or without accompaniment.

staccato   Italian, from *staccare* (to detach). Short notes to be played crisply and separately without *legato* and indicated by dots above the notes.

symphony   Originally an instrumental passage in a choral work. The name was sometimes applied to overtures or pieces played during the intervals in theaters. Finally, the name was given to orchestral compositions (sometimes with voices added) in sonata form.

terzi tuoni   Italian, meaning third tones. Also known as differential or combination tones. An overtone that is sounded when the string player stops two tones. The pitch is the difference in frequency of the two stopped tones.

transcriptions   Name given to compositions adapted from one form to another, such as a piano version of a song.

tutti   Italian, meaning, literally all. A musical passage played or sung by all the performers together.

vibrato   Italian, from *vibrare* (to vibrate). An effect used by singers and string players in which a note is sung or played so that it pulsates, giving greater warmth and intensity. String players produce *vibrato* by rocking the finger on a string, thereby producing slight variations in pitch.

viol   A bowed, six-stringed instrument of the sixteenth and seventeenth centuries.

virtuoso   Italian, from *virtu* (virtue or superiority). Name given to performers of extraordinary talent and skill.

Index